In Clear and Present Danger

BY JOHN W. CAUGHEY   **In Clear**

and Present Danger

The Crucial State of Our Freedoms

THE UNIVERSITY OF CHICAGO PRESS

Library of Congress Catalogue No. 58-10815

THE UNIVERSITY OF CHICAGO PRESS, CHICAGO 37
Cambridge University Press, London, N.W. 1, England
The University of Toronto Press, Toronto 5, Canada

© 1958 by The University of Chicago. Published 1958
Composed and printed by THE UNIVERSITY OF CHICAGO PRESS
Chicago, Illinois, U.S.A.

To LaRee

Preface

When the Russians startled the West by putting the first satellites into orbit, Secretary of State Dulles warned that in order to retain "our larger freedom" we might have to "give up small marginal freedoms."

By the "larger freedom" he clearly meant our national security. No one can be indifferent to that interest. This book is not. It is, however, addressed to the liberties that are small and marginal: freedom of religion, of speech and assembly, of the press, the freedom of the individual against arbitrary duress by his government, and the freedoms contained in the guaranties of due process.

In the context of the postwar years Dulles' remark was hardly more than a commonplace, so far have we gone in surrendering the traditional personal freedoms in order to keep up the instalments on security. That march of events is the subject matter of this book, with some analysis of why we moved so far in this direction in the era of McCarthy and how much these abridgments of freedom came to be taken for granted and given permanence.

The moons of Khrushchev, totalitarian though they are, may have the ironic consequence of heralding more freedom as well as more money for American science. There is much less reason to expect that their magic will produce a general revitalizing of the freedoms in the United States. As of this writing—under the sign of Sputnik though it is—the evidence is that the state of our civil liberties still is critical. Hence the title.

Some of the writing toward this book began eight or ten years ago. Parts appeared, though in substantially different form, in *Frontier, Harper's,* and the *Bulletin of the American Association of University Professors,* but recasting continued, and the perspective is emphatically post-McCarthy. I had the fortune to be close to a number of the episodes and to know several of the people involved. Consequently, although the book is not shaped or intended as a personal testament, toward much of its content I do have a feeling of identification.

I imposed on several friends, would-be publishers, and members of my family to read the manuscript in whole or in part. I particularly thank A. L. Wirin and Eason Monroe, two most devoted laborers for civil liberty. For help at all stages and for unlimited encouragement I owe the most to LaRee, my wife.

J. W. C.

Contents

1. Our Bartered Freedoms

For the United States in the 1930's no phrase seemed more apt than "It can't happen here." Round about us, other peoples were turning back the clock and submitting to the highhanded discipline and terror of dictatorial governments. The Germans were responding like robots to der Führer and the Italians to il Duce. The Japanese and the Russians were accepting regimentation under other forms of totalitarianism. But as for us, we had the comfortable assurance that democracy was here to stay.

The time was only yesterday. Most adult Americans can recall it. Yet in this rapidly aging world that era now seems unbelievably remote. It was prewar and preatomic, and in other respects virtually prehistoric. Almost unanimously we then had high confidence in the fundamentals of the American system. By our Constitution and its Bill of Rights we were dedicated to equality before the law and respect for the dignity of the individual. These honored principles had not always been perfectly realized in practice. The blows struck by the Alien and Sedition Acts in the 1790's are one black mark on the American conscience. Yesterday's persecution of the Wobblies, the lawlessness of the Palmer raids, and the hooded violence of the Ku Klux Klan are other examples. Yet it seemed unthinkable that we would desert

1

the pledged ideal of "liberty and justice for all" and deliberately turn to authoritarianism of any brand.

This confidence held up remarkably well during the Second World War. With the exception of what was done to the Japanese Americans—an enormity of an exception, it must be admitted—this great and hard war was fought with very little abridgment of the freedoms in the United States.

After the war the panic started. The postwar years were perplexing. Crisis followed crisis in rapid succession, and the gravity of the threats seemed to call for extraordinary countermeasures. Repeatedly we were told that to save our society we must set aside part of the traditional protection of the individual. The figure of speech, the Cold War, was used to justify abridgments such as had appeared in times of declared and actual war. Fighting fire with fire became the excuse for totalitarian methods in the defense of the free world.

At first, there was frank admission that elements of our heritage of freedom were being sacrificed. The excuse was expediency, and there was the sugar-coating that the retirement of a time-honored freedom was to be strictly temporary. Yet as the crises multiplied and refused to down, we found ourselves thrust into a state of continuous emergency. Measures that were to have been only for the moment thus came to be perpetuated.

Throughout it has been the fashion to speak contemptuously of the more blatant leaders in the assaults on the freedoms. We have criticized their excesses and their sensationalism. We have censured their callous unconcern about damage to the innocent. With one accord we deplore the crudities of these political hacks and rabble-rousers. This disclaimer has become a ritual, a twentieth-century washing of the hands. Yet in the next breath, many have gone on to say that, after all, these wild men were doing a job that had to be done. They were fingering suspects, exposing doubtful characters, rooting out potential traitors, silencing dissent, and forcing political conformity. Such pious ejaculations salved the conscience and all too often led to acceptance of methods and measures known to be destructive of the institutions of freedom.

No one would contend that the United States in the postwar era went completely totalitarian. Yet the things that we did and the things we allowed to be done put America's traditional freedoms in clear and present danger. Those words, of course, belong to Justice Holmes. Supposing an instance in a crowded theater in which a man might cry "Fire, fire," he asserted that on occasions of "clear and present danger" the Constitutional guaranty of freedom of speech could not hold. This doctrine is debatable. The case under trial did not involve any such irresponsible outcry and Holmes's argument did not persuade the court. Subsequently his dictum has been stretched to cover cases of clouded and remote danger and thus to undercut the Bill of Rights.

This narrowing of our freedom can be seen in laws enacted, orders given, cases decided, and congressional and administrative behavior. What the government has done is momentous. What individual demagogues in and out of the government have done may be even more significant. Yet these matters are hardly more than surface indications of a current that runs much deeper. There has been a contagion of demogoguery, a subversion of faith in the democratic way. We are confronted with the saddening fact that a regime of freedom, of "liberty and justice for all," is not as safe in the hearts of the rank and file of Americans as it was even half a generation ago.

Indeed, a case can be made that the plight of the freedoms has never been so critical. Refinements in methods of interfering with these freedoms such as never occurred to our less adroit ancestors have become commonplace. Because the freedoms are less practiced, they have retreated into theory. What is worse, many of us seem to have lost faith and view them with distrust. Reporters who should know and, in 1955, Chief Justice Warren, who is not given to exaggerations, have questioned whether the Bill of Rights, if it were not already in the Constitution, would get the necessary votes for adoption.

3

The evidence of intimidation, inroads, and lowered faith is mountainous. The greater part of it, furthermore, has piled up in the last few years. Anti-Communism, the guise under which the most serious inroads on the freedoms have occurred, was no more than an incidental issue in the presidential campaign of 1948, and as recently as January, 1950, Senator McCarthy had not discovered the Communist issue.

In the spring of 1950 the Senate was exhibiting a healthy skepticism about McCarthy's charge that there were Communists in the State Department. By that time, it is true, President Truman had proclaimed his program for the loyalty screening of federal employees, the Attorney-General had issued his list of suspect organizations, the House Un-American Activities Committee had cut a swath through Hollywood, academic freedom had suffered a reverse at the University of Washington and was getting another at the University of California, and the Board of Supervisors at Los Angeles had voted to remove Communist books from the Los Angeles County Library. There were other threats to freedom, but they were scattered and sporadic. At this stage it was still possible to keep track of the casualties.

The counsel often given was to roll with the punches, to wait for a more auspicious time for striking back, to soft-pedal on protest, and to back-pedal on resistance. Something of the sort might have been prudent, but as the couplet ought to read:

> He who fights and runs away
> Will live to run another day.

Within the next few years the assaults broadened. The State Department, prodded by McCarthy, stooped to book-burning. The House Un-American Activities Committee traduced the good name of Bishop G. Bromley Oxnam. In the Los Angeles school system, the second largest in the nation, the school board scuttled the study of UNESCO. The veterans at Norwalk set themselves up as little G men. McCarthy went on the warpath against the Army—and won several battles. The Attorney-General offered accusation as a sufficient substitute for trial and conviction. Unscrupulous politicians stretched the doctrine of guilt by association to the point of calling the opposition the party of treason. They resorted to a numbers racket and falsely claimed 1,456, then 2,427, then 8,008 subversives discharged from federal jobs. A group of university presidents banded together and abrogated the Fifth Amendment insofar as the faculties of their schools were concerned. The California legislature sublet inquisitorial power to school boards. On the basis of charges not yet evaluated, the President withdrew the security clearance of the chief architect of the atomic bomb and ordered "a blank wall" put between him and all secret plans and formulas. The Atomic Energy Commission made the suspension permanent. Then there was the spectacle of a congressional subcommittee sitting in pretended judgment upon itself, and of McCarthy calling on government employees not to let the labels "classified" or "top secret" deter them from passing information on to him and his committee. Shortly thereafter he denounced the senators who recommended his censure as "handmaidens of Communism." For these antics the Senate reprimanded him, but McCarthyism marched on. The Justice Department lodged an accusation of bias against the federal judge who had set aside two of the counts in the first indictment of Owen Lattimore, and the Department of Agriculture tried to justify the dismissal of Wolf Ladejinsky on the ground that in words and in action he had been anti-Communist. Senator Eastland's hazing of the New York *Times* was as venomous as McCarthy's earlier move against the New York *Post* and claimed a much larger toll in dismissals and citations for contempt. Early in 1957, when his appointment to the Supreme Court was up for confirmation, Justice Brennan quailed before McCarthy and backtracked on his earlier criticism of witch hunting. In March, 1957, when Dave Beck stood on the Fifth Amendment, President Eisenhower volunteered that whenever anyone refused to testify he could not help believing that it was because he had something to hide. This remark was from the highest officer of the land, who just a couple of months earlier had renewed his oath to up-

5

hold the Constitution. It illustrated and emphasized how pervasive the popular abridgment of the freedoms had become.

In the broad context of our national history, this cumulative battering of the freedoms has an air of unreality about it. It fits Shakespeare's lines,

> If this were played upon a stage now,
> I would condemn it as an improbable fiction.

By looking just slightly beneath the surface, however, it is possible to see how this astounding degradation came about. One clear reason is that the pattern of our life has altered most drastically since the days of Washington and Jefferson. The population, which has pyramided to some 170,000,000 souls, presses upon the resources of the land. This growth in numbers has cut down the elbowroom, while changes in the technology of production, distribution, and business have made us far more interrelated.

Accompanying these shifts has come a change in our philosophy of government. Gone is the doctrine that the best government is the one that governs least. Instead, we encourage the government to hold and manage vast parks and forest reserves, to build and operate great hydroelectric plants, to enter the insurance business, and to launch upon countless other undertakings. We also look to the government, especially at the national level, to regulate a great many activities that once would have been left to the discretion of the individual or firm.

The bipartisan support that this trend has had is one indication of its virtual inevitability. The financial reforms of the Wilson era and the complex of activities that we call the New Deal were major elements in its rise. But the Republican Roosevelt yielded to none as an enthusiast for conservation and trustbusting; another Republican, George Norris, fathered the TVA; and Herbert Hoover's RFC initiated the New Deal. Many Republicans, it is true, have tried to dissociate themselves from this trend. It is standard practice for the conservatives to rant about "Creeping Socialism." Yet, when confronted with the responsibility of governing, these same conservatives are hesitant about turning back the clock by reducing government services or dismantling controls. In its first years in office, the Eisenhower administration softened many consumer-protecting restraints on private business, severely cut back supports for public housing, backed away from public power projects, and made rate, development, and tax concessions to private utility corporations. Yet the grand total of governmental operation was not perceptibly reduced in volume or cost. Conservatives as well as liberals take an active and pervasive government for granted.

Furthermore, we have today a sense of crisis. On the domestic front, taxes and the national debt are at an all-time high. According to one calculation the average American has to work for the government until April 27 before he can turn to earning for himself and his family. Bureaucracy seems overlarge. Buoyed up by the program of aid to our allies and by the growing armaments race, our over-all economy flourishes. Yet there are sick industries, as, for example, watchmaking and motion-picture production. Inflation has victimized those who are dependent on savings and fixed income. And with the depression of the thirties still a painful memory, we cannot put out of mind the possibility of another descent to the bottom of the business cycle.

Meanwhile, in the realm of international relations, we find ourselves confronted by a strange opponent—ponderous, resourceful, implacable, and by our standards unprincipled. The size, stamina, and firepower of Russia impress us as formidable, but there are other things about the Soviets that trouble us more. They seem not to be bound by the rules of diplomacy or by the laws of economics. Also, although there may be more unrest behind the Iron Curtain than is certified to us, the Soviets seem to be able to marshal full support in Russia and close to full support in the satellite countries. This is the nation with which it is our lot to coexist.

Furthermore, this fearsome and mysterious foe darkens the horizon much too soon after the last great war. That war, in which we went all out to get rid of totalitarianism, so weakened our "natural" allies, particularly Britain and France, that they are far less able to bear an effective hand against the new menace. In something like desperation we have turned, then, to an "unnatural" alliance with the likes of Franco and to pinning our hopes on a rearmed Germany and Japan.

We too were depleted by the Second World War. In physical respects, notwithstanding the tragic toll of killed and wounded, it hardly shows. In fact, we emerged with more wherewithal for waging war than we had in 1941. Nevertheless, as to stomach for war, inevitably there is less of it. Consequently, the Dulles diplomacy of repeatedly taking us to the brink of war has never been popular, and the Eisenhower doctrine guaranteeing the status quo in the Middle East appears to draw a longer bow than we possess.

As if our domestic problems and the gravity of the Russian menace were not enough, we also find ourselves threatened by a runaway science. From the airplane, high explosives, blockbusters, guided missiles, and other such refinements, science has gone on to split the atom and to unleash destructive forces infinitely more dreadful than any that mankind previously had to face. Winston Churchill may be right that they are so awesome that neither side will dare to use them. From the Soviets, however, we expect no such self-restraint. And as to ourselves, having already broken through this moral barrier with the bombs dropped at Hiroshima and Nagasaki, we can no longer say that it is a question of whether we will use such a weapon but merely of how much or how little provocation we will wait for.

How devastating an atomic war would be, the average man does not know and cannot know. A formidable array of scientific opinion warns against continuation of our testing of atomic and hydrogen bombs. The administration assures that the limits of safety are not being exceeded. Yet with many scientists unpersuaded, the specter of catastrophe remains to haunt us.

Judging from the outward appearance, we Americans have taken in stride these three menaces: a greater depression, war with Russia, and an atomic holocaust. To a great extent, we have gone about our daily affairs with business as usual, life as usual, and politics as usual. Beneath this stoical calm, however, we have developed what amounts to a national passion for security. On the economic front it shows through with such programs as social security and other retirement systems, an expanded civil service, seniority rights to employment, guaranteed bank deposits, so-called fair trade practices putting floors under retail prices, and price support for farm products. On the international front this passion for security led us to permit the military and the general in the White House practically to write their own ticket on defense spending. On the atomic front it has gone a long way toward making the resort to atomic warfare only a tactical decision. Any remaining doubts on this point were erased by the Eisenhower administration's New Look, its promise of "massive retaliation," and its insistence on going ahead with H-bomb testing.

The unquestioning attitude when security is allegedly involved goes still further. On this altar of security Americans have been persuaded to sacrifice the freedoms. The record is inescapable that such sacrifices have been made and that they involve practically every freedom.

Freedom of religion, for example, was shaken in J. B. Matthews' blanket charge that seven thousand Protestant clergymen were servants of Communism, and in Congressman Donald Jackson's accusation that Bishop Oxnam served God on Sunday and Communism the rest of the week. When Congressman Velde announced that his committee would probe into disloyalty in the churches, there was such a protest from the public that the committee decided not to pursue the matter after all. On the other hand, when Senator McCarthy, without producing any evidence, impugned the loyalty of the late Rabbi Stephen S. Wise and Rabbi Judah L. Magnes, the protests were so scattered as to be ineffective. A California enactment requiring a test oath from churches as a condition for continued tax exemption is a bald move to subordinate church to state. These are merely random examples of the current tendency, in the name of security, to violate freedom of religion, a tendency which alarmed many churchmen. The General Council of the Presbyterian Church saw fit to address a letter of analysis and warning to the two and a half million members of this denomination.

Freedom of speech has been a more common target. First it was a matter of denying platforms to known members of the Communist party. Then the objection spread to the broader and vaguer category of fellow travelers, as when the University of California at Los Angeles canceled a lecture by Harold J. Laski. More recently, as when the Temple Baptist Church in Los Angeles refused to rent its auditorium for a Bishop Oxnam speech on the Bill of Rights, the excuse has been merely that a speaker was "controversial." We have gone a long way from the ideal said to have been voiced by Voltaire, "I disapprove of what you say, but I will defend to the death your right to say it."

Many of the interferences with freedom of speech have been by private groups or individuals. Others have been by countenance of the government, and this in spite of the Constitutional provision that "Congress shall make no law . . . abridging freedom of speech" and the similar ban that holds with regard to the state governments. There is no tally on how many speeches have gone unsaid and how many listeners were denied the opportunity to hear, but the grand total would be distressingly large.

Freedom of the press is another major area endangered. Since newspaper publication not only is big business but battens on big business advertising, we have come perilously close to having a one-party press. When, in addition, persons high in the government wage a deliberate campaign against papers which criticize them, freedom of the press is seriously threatened. Examples are Velde's mistaken charges against Mrs. Agnes E. Meyer of the Washington *Post*, McCarthy's blasts against the Madison *Times*, the Washington *Post*, and the St. Louis *Post-Dispatch* and, in particular, his hazing of James Wechsler and the New York *Post*. The most alarming thing about the Wechsler episode is that when it was referred for study to a committee of eleven newspapermen, only four could see that there had been an attack on freedom of the press. At a distance and in the abstract, however, all were for freedom of the press; no American editor condoned Perón's suppression of *La Prensa*.

Freedom to publish and freedom to read depend at least as significantly on magazines, books, and libraries. Here too the heavy hand of political censorship has made itself felt, and almost always with regard to publications thought to be too liberal. Thus the *Nation* and the *New Republic* have been removed from many public or school library shelves, and there have been moves to cull suspect volumes from certain libraries or to brand them "subversive." Some of these forays were blocked; others were not. Under pressure from McCarthy, the State Department not only withdrew a number of books from its overseas libraries but actually burned certain of them.

The state of Texas pursued the matter of purity of authorship one step further. By law no book can be used in the public schools of that state unless the author files an oath that he is not a Communist. If an author is no longer living—Shakespeare, for example—the publisher must file an oath on his behalf. By comparison, the patriotic lady in Indiana who wanted *Robin Hood* withdrawn from the shelves is less ridiculous, for Robin Hood and his Merrie Men levied on the rich to distribute to the poor. And that, by one definition, is the worst sort of un-Americanism.

Likewise in the newer media of communication the hysteria over security has curtailed freedom of expression. Whatever opportunity the most despised minority in the country, the Communists, might have had to use these channels was long since rescinded, partly by governmental action, partly by private. Alleged fellow travelers and alleged associates with Communists were next brought under scrutiny. Practically everyone thus suspected has been put off the air and the picture waves, out of the movies, and out of commission for other functioning in the arts. Commentators with liberal leanings are in constant hot water. In some instances it has been documented that reactionary pressure groups built the fire with a barrage of letters, phone calls, and threats of boycott. If such groups could have their way, we would have a one-party radio, television, and cinema. That the networks are jumpy was demonstrated early in 1957 when C.B.S. suppressed an Eric Sevareid commentary on Dulles' handling of the crisis in the Middle East.

Political censorship is also rampant in the realm of the arts and literature. Thus the county supervisors in Los Angeles took alarm over a mural in their meeting hall. The long leather hunting shirts of the pioneer American fur trappers looked to some of the supervisors like Russian tunics, and they considered having this picture blotted out. A comparable commotion was raised about the murals in the Rincon Post Office in San Francisco. Too much of the seamier side of early California is portrayed to please one school of thought on how local history should be presented, and the protectors of the tradition wanted this art work discarded. Their art criticism was essentially political. Another example was the last-minute refusal at the University of California at Los Angeles to exhibit the José Clemente Orozco paintings and drawings that were on tour in 1953. The reason as publicized was that in some of his work this great artist used Communist symbols.

Along with freedom of religion, speech, and the press, the First Amendment guarantees freedom to assemble and peaceably to petition the government for redress of grievances. The broad intent would seem to be that Americans should be free to associate with one another as they might choose, and specifically with political purpose. For a time we entered upon this part of our heritage with such enthusiasm that foreign visitors characterized us as a nation of joiners. That day is no more. The FBI and legislative investigating committees, freely assisted by the private dossier-peddlers, have made us as a people aware that associating and joining are hazardous in the extreme. Today the average citizen is hesitant about signing petitions. In donating to a good cause he often prefers to send cash rather than a traceable check. For a people as free as we still consider ourselves to be, all this seems fantastic; yet it is true that anyone who might later want to apply for a government job, a passport, or even for a position with a concern holding government contracts could have old associations held against him, especially if they had anything of a liberal tinge to them. Even George F. Babbitt might have come a cropper over guilt by association as assigned today. It certainly discourages association in general.

Another freedom once well rooted in American life has also been undermined. The general name is civil service, but with it we may well lump the tenure system developed for public school teachers. Both were set up on the merit basis. The gist of the arrangement was that, after merit had been proved in a probationary period, there would be a presumption of permanent appointment, subject, however, to continued adequate performance and good character. Relatively few teachers and civil servants have been dismissed on other than the authorized grounds, but a number have been, and in circumstances that shake the whole system.

With security considerations as the announced justification, the millions of citizens in these employments have been required to take a whole series of test oaths, have been subjected to elaborate loyalty checks, and some have been haled up to answer unspecified charges from unidentified informants. By executive order and by state law the Fifth Amendment has been revoked for most of these people, and with it the presumption of innocence. Instead, the burden of proving innocence rests upon the public employee. In a very real sense, therefore, they have become second-class citizens. They have been reminded, too, that public employment is a privilege, not a right. This maxim has a surface accuracy, but, pushed to the hilt, it would absolutely destroy civil service and teacher tenure.

Comparable inroads have been made on academic freedom, primarily through special test oath requirements, subjecting teachers and scholars to grilling by legislative committees or in imitation thereof by school authorities, retracting the Fifth

Amendment, and invoking the so-called doctrine of guilt by association.

These attacks on scholars suspected of Communist party membership, on others who are charged with associations with Communists, and on still others who are allegedly "insubordinate" or "controversial" have been the cutting edge of the drive on academic freedom. Alongside has come a more general blighting, widely attested to, in which scholars and teachers have become less venturesome, less willing to pursue the truth when it leads toward unpopular conclusions, less willing to provoke thought on the part of their students, less willing to face up to issues that are controversial, and much less willing to belong to any but the most innocuous of community groups.

Then there is a cluster of freedoms that we used to regard as minimum rights for all persons who live in America. Among them are such matters as freedom of movement, including until recently the right to travel abroad, protection against search and seizure without warrant, arrest without cause, ex post facto laws, unreasonable bail, trial without due process, and cruel or unusual punishments. The list is much longer. In sum, it amounts to an insistence on proper respect for the individual and a guaranty against a descent to police state methods.

In our day nobody openly advocates the setting-up of a police state; yet with security as the watchword there has been a substantial whittling away at some of these rights. For example, wire-tapping and eavesdropping by ingeniously planted "bugs" now constitute a considerable invasion of privacy. If Attorney-General Brownell had had his way, there would have been much more of it. The passport policies of the government have set a political curb on the right to travel. The strictures on Charlie Chaplin are in sharpest contrast to the right of asylum which Washington extended to Citizen Genêt, even though he had been engaged in open subversion. The bail requirements in recent trials of Communist leaders have been high, and some on appeal have been ruled excessive. The file-building techniques of the FBI, at least as we have been given to understand them, are a far remove from the old rules of evidence. The loyalty board hearings with their anonymous and unspecified charges are an undercutting of due process, and the same can be said of the hearings before legislative investigating committees, which in many instances have stood in lieu of regular trial in court.

Another group of freedoms crucially important to the functioning of our democratic republic consists of those that might be called political. Although with remissness in practice as to the Negro in parts of the South, we have zealously upheld as an ideal the right of the individual to register as he pleases, to advocate any candidate, party, or measure without fear of reprisal, and to cast a secret ballot. We do not tolerate prying into the politics of an employee or prospective employee. We try to keep the civil service free of politics and, more important, to keep politics free of any such delivery of a bloc of votes. Yet when Communism enters the picture, we discard all this idealism. By almost every measure short of completely outlawing it we have read the Communist party out of existence. Those who worked for Wallace in 1948 or for the IPP in 1952 are not much better off, not to mention the hundreds of organizations, political and otherwise, on the Attorney-General's list.

The Lucille Ball affair, though exceptional in that it had a happy ending, illustrates the decline of political freedom. The "crime" alleged was that in 1936 she had registered as a Communist. For a time it seemed that "I Love Lucy" would be lost to television and that Metro-Goldwyn-Mayer would not be able to release a multimillion-dollar picture that it had completed. These investments were saved, but only after Miss Ball was put through an ignominious ordeal.

First, she had to explain away the act of registering. It was a youthful indiscretion, she said, done in filial piety to please her grandfather. Second, her husband felt that he had to broadcast that Lucille should not be held responsible because she was really a dumbbell so far as politics was concerned. Third, it was argued that she must be all right: she had voted for Eisenhower. This young woman escaped with her career, but only after she was brought to tears, worry, and humiliation out of all proportion to the error of her ways, if that is what it was. The incident reveals how zeal for security has made substantial inroads on the political freedom that once existed.

Out of this incomplete catalogue of the sacrifices of freedom on the altar of security, the question inevitably arises, What do we mean by security?

We mean, first of all, that our country be protected against attack from without. Toward that end we maintain military forces and, through the State Department and the United Nations, we mount a diplomacy whose purpose is to reduce the likelihood of any such attack. Through armaments and allies we also try to put ourselves in position to repel such an attack if it should come. The formula on which we rely for security against external danger calls for a huge investment in armament and in trained fighting men, a stand-by arsenal in field and factory that can in emergency pour out all the sinews of war, and a diplomacy that will give us some choice about when and where we fight and not alone. Even with the advantage of being a continent apart from the nation that menaces us, this formula calls for almost ruinous contributions. We have to be reconciled to the fact, too, that no matter how much we do we will not have absolute security.

If there existed another nation with ideals and institutions exactly like ours, we still would not want to be conquered by it. Our present worry about the threat from without is, however, very much aggravated by recognition that Soviet Russia has theories and methods diametrically different from ours, and that, should the Soviets gain sway over the United States, the American way of life and our cherished institutions would certainly die. The Soviets, we take it for granted, would wipe out most private property rights and would impose state control on agriculture, industry, and business.

Beyond these generalities we specifically fear that Soviet conquest would mean that a police state would be set up, making arbitrary arrests, conducting secret trials, canceling the protection of due process of law, and imposing heavy and heartless punishments. Free political choice would disappear; those who dared oppose the group in power would be purged; elections would become a farce; the independence of legislative, executive, and judicial branches would disappear, and along with it any possibility of freedom of decision in state and local government. Such a regime would suppress freedom of religion, and of speech or press except for voicing the authorized and orthodox views. Radio, television, and the schools would become mere agencies of indoctrination and propaganda for the declared orthodoxy. Under statism the individual would be reduced to insignificance, would lose the authorization to think for himself, to decide where to work or on what terms, or to exercise any other initiative or assertiveness. Totalitarians may relish such a system, but to us it looks like a government over the people, on the people, and against the people.

The basic purpose of the external phase of our security program stands out clearly. It ought to be equally apparent that the domestic phase of the program should try to uphold exactly the same set of values. Here likewise it is not just our lives but our freedoms as individuals that we want saved, and that is the fundamental justification of the internal as well as the external part of the security program.

When we talk about internal security, however, confusion sets in. A program so labeled has two possible assignments. One is to take precautions against activities within the nation—espionage, sabotage, or treason, to be explicit—that would contribute toward the success of an attack from abroad. The other possible assignment is to guard against an attack from within—specifically a rebellion or a revolution.

In line with the purpose immortalized by Gilbert and Sullivan "to make the punishment fit the crime," we can insist that the internal security program should "make the precaution fit the peril." In the present crusade against Communism much that has been done on the home front violates this rule.

At no time in the era of the Cold War have the Communists

17

been on the verge of taking over in the United States. Their voice in the press and on the air is exceedingly small. They do not have the schools or the churches in their hands. If a single Communist holds office it is only because he has concealed his identity. Of all Americans they are the least likely to succeed in gaining any important following. Their chances of taking over the United States were never good, and the menace of such a take-over is now the wildest sort of fantasy.

This, nevertheless, is the improbability against which the bulk of the internal security action has been directed: the silencing of speech, writing, and argument that might have the appearance of being pro-Communist; requirement of anti-Communist oaths from tens of millions of Americans; an elaborate and expensive probe into the "loyalty coefficient" of every federal employee no matter how non-sensitive his position; legislative committee probes into labor, education, the press, the church, and the entertainment industry; and, for a host of individuals, a reduction of the rights of due process, presumption of innocence, and of freedom of speech, religion, assembly, and political association. Insofar as these invasions of the freedoms were intended as precautions against our becoming converts to Communism, they are utterly without justification, and as controls on the handful of committed Communists they have little more excuse.

Yet they are less illogical than our folly of trying to maintain our security by destroying it piecemeal—of trying to keep freedom bright in America by turning off the lights one by one. The real bulwark of our republic, in Alan Barth's happy phrase, is "the loyalty of free men." True security will be ours only as we keep each of the freedoms intact.

2. The Birthright

Our forefathers who in Lincoln's phrase "brought forth upon this continent a new nation" gave us a noble heritage of freedom. They did it when in wealth and power and political experience the United States was one of the least among the nations. For the Founding Fathers still to be willing to give full play to the freedoms was, therefore, an act of high courage. Now, by almost every measure, the United States has attained great strength. For us at such a time to debase the practice and doctrine of liberty is paradoxical. It also bears the stamp of cowardice.

In this ignoble betrayal, furthermore, we have made far more than a personal sacrifice. What we have been doing is much more frightening. Whether we realize it or not, in surrendering the freedoms, piece by piece, we have betrayed our birthright. We have been undermining the very foundation of our system of government and most seriously imperiling its chances for survival.

What is this birthright?

Because America is so large and complex, thoughtful men have not always agreed as to its essence. Some have been most impressed with the distinctive features of its government. They note the experiment with federalism, an ingenious system allocating certain powers to the nation and others to the states, and making every resident directly answerable to both parts of this dual government. They note another and more venturesome experiment—again for the first time in a nation of any considerable size—the choice of the democratic-republican form. Under it, in theory and in ultimate fact, it is the people who are sovereign.

Other observers, less political-minded, see as the vital fact the peopling of the continent with stocks drawn from every quarter of the globe and the welding of these strains into what amounts to a new race. Still others stress the transplanting of Western civilization to this new environment and emphasize the cultural indebtedness.

A more engaging interpretation is that America spells opportunity. From earliest times men have seen it as a land of promise. They have believed that it held out the offer of a richer living. Sometimes, it must be admitted, the New World has not measured up to these expectations. The first comers to Virginia, for example, suffered famine and pestilence, and as recently as the Great Depression the bounteous quality of America seemed reduced to a mockery. Viewed in the long range, however, America has proved plentiful beyond the dream. The well-being that has been achieved is valid ground for pride; yet opportunity in the purely materialistic sense is not the full reason for our feeling for our country.

Beginning in the colonial period and in swelling volume thereafter, millions of persons registered faith in this land by migrating to these shores. The reasons for their coming offer at least a clue to the meaning of America. In practically every instance there was a combination of motives, and almost always the hope ran beyond mere creature comforts.

Many of the colonists, as is well known, turned to America to find refuge from religious or political persecution. In the nineteenth century other thousands came for asylum from militarism and from overbearing governments. Economic advantages were prized; yet when the American welcome was symbolized it was by a goddess holding aloft not the full dinner pail but the torch of freedom.

Millions, indeed tens of millions, accepting this welcome, fortified America in numbers, and, more important, in grateful loyalty. The quota system enacted in 1924 and the harsher mechanics of the McCarran Acts have barred many of the gates. These laws modify the present and future course of the nation. They cannot eradicate its historic character as a shelter for the oppressed and the persecuted.

An even better indication of the soul of America may lie in the sentiments that are most familiar. Phrases such as "America the beautiful," "land of plenty," and "the American standard of living" express our carnal appreciation. Other phrases are more warming and more at the heart of the matter: "sweet land of liberty," "let freedom ring," "the land of the free," "with liberty and justice for all," that all men are endowed with certain "unalienable rights" among which are "life, liberty and the pursuit of happiness," "that this nation, under God, shall have a new birth of freedom—and that government of the people, by the people, and for the people shall not perish from the earth."

At the essence it is something on this order that America brings to mind. It is not just by accident that we have a Liberty Bell; that the climax of the national anthem—the place where one soprano takes over alone—is with the words "land of the free"; or that our most cherished state papers, the Declaration of Independence and the Gettysburg Address, boldly pronounce that our nation was "conceived in liberty" and is "dedicated to the proposition that all men are created equal."

These noble phrases carry a double message. They voice our devotion to the freedoms, stating a lofty idealism that is pleasant to contemplate and inspiring to the mind. They are equally emphatic in asserting a thoroughgoing respect for the dignity of the individual. They insist that each and every person, the least as well as the greatest, shall be free from arbitrary restraints.

A moment's thought makes clear that these two elements are as the two sides of a coin. The general theme of the freedoms is our guiding principle. But if these freedoms are to be more than philosophical they must be applied in human affairs, which means that all men must be equally eligible for their benefits. The one is freedom in theory; the other, freedom in fact.

Thus it may be that the noblest of all these phrases are the ones in which the freedoms are given a down-to-earth application. Thus also the real palladium of the freedoms, the special place where they are made specific and particular, is the Bill of Rights, the first ten amendments to the Constitution. There one finds the bans against governmental interference with freedom of religion, speech, the press, and assembly. These amendments also put the shield of the Constitution around every individual. They protect him against unreasonable search and seizure, against being penalized without due process of law, against trial without presentment of charges or without witnesses and assistance of counsel. They protect him against double jeopardy, forced self-incrimination, excessive bail, or cruel and unusual punishments. This is not the whole catalogue of Constitutional guaranties, but it is enough to illustrate the fundamental concern that the freedoms shall be a tangible reality.

These explicit guaranties of freedom incarnate were not in the Constitution as drafted at Philadelphia. The Convention took the line that rights such as these were so elementary that no government would dare to invade them. In the debate over ratification wiser counsel prevailed. The case for setting these guaranties forth in black and white was argued by a number of men, including some of the chief authors of the Constitution, and most eloquently by Thomas Jefferson. These men deserve our everlasting gratitude. With little delay the First Congress drew up and voted the amendments and the states quickly ratified them.

The ideas contained in the Bill of Rights, however, were not sudden inventions. On the contrary, they stemmed from the philosophy of the age and from American political experience.

By the late eighteenth century the political theory of the

divine right of kings was much discounted. The preferred belief was that governments were created by men and existed for the benefit of the people concerned. Thus, the Declaration of Independence forcibly stated that if a government flagrantly violates its trust, the people are justified in setting it aside. This proposition is just the opposite of the totalitarian doctrine that the state has priority over the people. To the authors of our Constitution and Bill of Rights, it was the individual rather than the state that was made in the image of God. When natural or inalienable rights were asserted, they were those of the individual.

The lessons of experience were just as explicit. Although England's American colonies had been nurtured on neglect, the behavior of appointed officers had made the colonials wary of executive and judicial authority. The legislative branch, through which there had been practice in self-government, was in somewhat better repute yet not altogether trusted because such bodies had often proved mere accessories to the governor. When King George and his ministers moved to grasp more revenue and more authority, the colonials became restive, and after the Revolution they still had a healthy skepticism about governments. "The price of liberty," said Jefferson, "is eternal vigilance," and he meant eternal vigilance against usurpations by government.

The further experience of the United States as a nation reinforced the freedom-loving philosophy of democracy. From the outset the frontier put special emphasis on self-reliance, individual initiative, and impatience with restraints. In the later advance of settlement across the continent, the frontier changed but did not lose this democratizing tendency. Long after the frontier of free land was gone, the tradition persisted. The successive waves of immigrants were another factor intensifying the emphasis on freedom.

In addition, there has been much purposeful extension of the meaning of freedom. The emancipation movement, the drive for women's rights, the recognition of public responsibility to provide for education, and the increasing concern about minority rights are examples of how the social gospel of democracy has been given greater depth of meaning. In some respects, thus, the content of American freedom is greater today than when the nation was launched.

All along we also have wanted to help other people achieve a comparable enjoyment of liberty. This attitude is expressed in our support of the United Nations. It is present in our concern about the peoples caught behind the Iron Curtain. It dates back to the beginning, as is indicated in Benjamin Franklin's prayer: "God grant that not only the love of liberty, but a thorough knowledge of the rights of man may pervade all the nations of the earth, so that a philosopher may set foot anywhere on its surface and say: This is my country."

With us the freedoms have the quality of copybook maxims. Therefore, we hold them to be "natural rights" which exist because of inexorable logic. To call them "divine rights" would have much the same meaning, but because that phrase was earlier appropriated by monarchism we seldom use it. Regarding the freedoms as appropriate to all mankind, we sometimes refer to them as "human rights." More often, in sincere compliment, which nonetheless gilds the lily, we call them "American rights." The freedoms, in point of fact, would pass as the national trademark.

Nevertheless, we often are shamefully unmindful of their fundamental nature and purpose. Since they are inherited, it is easy to take them for granted. Because they are traditional, their wording is sometimes archaic, and their names, like most names, stop short of full definition. Because they operate in the realm of law, some of them are quite technical in phrasing and functioning. Factors such as these help to account for the confusion that exists. To re-examine the freedoms and work out a clearer definition of what they involve would be a real service.

The most significant catalogue, of course, is in the Constitution. A point to note is that everything said there about the freedoms is in terms of what the government shall or shall not do. "Congress shall make no law" are the words that herald most of these guaranties. No such legislation being permitted, the executive branch of government cannot enforce any such restrictions and the courts cannot uphold them. The government thus is effectively forbidden certain actions that would be detrimental or ruinous to the freedoms. Frequently these provisions have broader consequence and mean that the government cannot aid or abet or countenance any such action. The approach of the Constitution may seem to be distressingly negative; yet perhaps the best way to make the government a champion of freedom is by eliminating it absolutely as a party to violations of particular freedoms.

Equally noteworthy is the fact that every one of these bans comes down to something that government is not permitted to do to any individual citizen or subject. They are in the form of protecting each and every person from domineering treatment at the hands of government. In terms of personal satisfaction these guaranteed freedoms are worth a great deal. To be assured against Gestapo-like arrests and manhandling, star-chamber convictions, and unjust punishments, and to be further assured against governmental interference with religion, expression, and political association, goes far toward meeting the basic requirements for satisfactory existence. There is good personal reason for every individual to cherish such freedoms.

Concern for the individual, however, is only part of the reason for setting up these guaranties. They have a social purpose at least as important. The Founding Fathers saw reasons of state for writing into the Constitution specific guaranties for the security of citizens.

In the United States as they fashioned it, the sovereign people govern in the main through elected and appointed representatives, to whom certain powers are delegated for a term of years or during faithful execution of the trust. Ultimate authority, however, rests with the people and with it the solemn responsibility of determining the fate of the nation. Certain of the guaranties written into the Constitution are there to make sure that we will continue to be in position to exercise this sovereignty. Or rather, as Alexander Meiklejohn has pointed out, these are freedoms which We the People, speaking through the Constitution, have reserved to ourselves. As sovereigns we have specifically forbidden our subordinates in government—the President, the Congress, and the courts—to abridge these freedoms which are so necessary for the proper exercise of our ultimate authority.

Seen in this light, some of the freedoms cease to be mere matters of personal privilege and become properties of society. For example, the sovereignty of the people must not be threatened by the dominance of any church. Therefore, the political functioning of the individual must not hinge on his being in or out of any particular church. In the context of popular sovereignty that is the rationale of freedom of religion.

Similarly, freedom to assemble is the authorization for the people to work together politically. Since it is inconceivable that any administration would interfere with those who organize in its support, the specific provision is that the people may assemble to petition for redress of grievances, that is, to criticize the existing regulations and administration and to advocate change.

In like manner, freedom of speech and freedom of the press have vital importance as means through which the people may be informed. On the surface these freedoms seem to hallow the soapbox and the pen. In a democratic republic such as ours, they exist for the speaker and the writer, but even more for the people as a whole. Because they assure that the people will not be shut off from ideas and opinions, these freedoms have special political significance and in a very real sense belong to society.

The standard phrasing of the freedoms does not make clear that society has a stake in them. The social significance would be better expressed if freedom of speech were known as freedom to hear; and freedom of the press, as freedom to read. The business end of these freedoms is the receiving end. Clearly these two freedoms are companion aspects of something larger—freedom to learn, to know, to make the best possible use of reason. Quite apart from its bearing on popular sovereignty this freedom, more formally known as "intellectual," and in the trade by the less appealing name "academic," stands as the summation and the keystone of the freedoms in general. It is the substance of Jefferson's ringing declaration, made, as we may be sure, with the sovereign people in mind, "I have sworn, upon the altar of God, eternal hostility to every form of tyranny over the mind of man."

This meaning of the freedoms is at the very heart of the meaning of America. It is the chief element in our birthright and the key to most that we cherish. Even more crucially, for us as a sovereign people it is the freedoms and they alone which can enable us to meet our responsibilities. To forfeit them or to allow them to be usurped is to fail in our duty under the Constitution. Rather, in this our land and this our system, to stand for freedom is an act of highest patriotism.

3. The Hue and Cry

In their palmiest days the Communists in America numbered a few hundred thousand, considerably less than 1 per cent of the grand total of Americans. From that peak the number has declined to the point where they are now no more than a trace element in the population. In influence and in prospects they have gone down even further. Nevertheless, in the postwar era we as a people have displayed more fear of Communism than of any other internal threat to the country. The cry of Red has been the sure-fire method of rousing passion and hate, and anti-Communism the one indispensable in politics.

With anti-Communism as the base line for all political planning and the surest footing for every appeal for popular support, it is small wonder that all sorts of voices have joined the chorus, or that the charge of being Communist or pro-Communist or soft on Communists has been hurled about with deliberate abandon. In fact, the hue and cry against Communism has become the leitmotif of modern America.

As with most such developments, a certain amount of historical causation can be detected. As long ago as 1789 the French Revolution had some of the features that we now identify with Communism. They, and the name as well, were even more prominent in the bloody uprising of the Paris Commune in 1870. In 1848, though without making much of an impression at the time, Karl Marx had published his *Communist Manifesto*, blueprinting the process whereby contrary governments and the capitalist system might be overthrown. In nineteenth-century Europe there were many critics of the prevailing social, economic, and political doctrines. Socialists advocated a benevolent statism. Anarchists, believing all government bad, were for the least possible degree of regulation. Communitarians practiced group withdrawal. Syndicalists put their faith in direct action and violence.

Through immigration and other forms of osmosis most of these ideas and labels crossed the Atlantic. They seldom, however, kept exactly the same meaning in the United States. Instead, American efforts at reform tended to develop a character and a philosophy of their own. They did so in the labor movement, in the various attempts to organize the farmers, and in most of the drives that produced third parties. A consequence was that European reform efforts seemed more foreign than they really were and that their exact meaning was often lost on Americans. Socialism, Anarchism, Nihilism, Syndicalism were all lumped together in popular thought and regarded as not for America. The designation "Red" was an easy carry-over, and the stage was set for the word "Communism" to be in the current speech a successor to all these terms and a catch-all for their quite diverse meanings.

The Russian Revolution, midway in the First World War, introduced a new factor. Because it supplanted the grinding and autocratic rule of the tsars and because it professed concern for the welfare of the common people, the new Russia initially had much to recommend it to Americans. Its totalitarian aspects were less evident at the outset, and its announced purpose of communizing the world could be discounted as propaganda for home consumption.

The blatant anticapitalism of the Soviets was grounds enough for the Harding, Coolidge, and Hoover administrations to withhold recognition. At the same time, the news from Russia was of ineptness, material setbacks, inefficiency in production and distribution, and enforced austerity. The total impression was that the Communist experiment was not working well enough to be much of a temptation to the rest of the world and certainly not to America.

The coming of the Great Depression fortified the Communist cause. It did not vindicate its positive program, but it raised serious doubts about the soundness of the economic policies of capitalism. Many Americans were convinced that a change was called for, and some saw the answer in Communism. The Communist party did gain recruits. That was not, however, the course which the nation elected. The New Deal was the reverse of Communism; it set itself to bolster and save the capitalist system.

In the thirties, furthermore, it seemed contrary to logic to point to Communism as the greatest menace to the world and to America. Immediately at hand was the depression, stubbornly resisting our best efforts to dispose of it. And, internationally, Communism was eclipsed by the more potent threat of Fascism, rampant in Germany, Italy, Spain, and Japan, and soon to engulf the world and us in an epic battle for survival. At the time, therefore, Communism was not in certainty the worst of all possible dangers.

The non-aggression pact between Hitler and Stalin at the start of the Second World War dealt a grave blow to Communist prestige in the United States. Hitler soon broke the pact and struck at Russia. As the Russians stubbornly and heroically fought back and, over the long pull, made a most substantial contribution to the defeat of Nazi Germany, American-Russian friendship seemed within the realm of possibility. Communism as such did not really gain in American favor, but Red and pro-Russian allegations lost some of their stigma. The optimism of V-E and V-J Days is now hard to recall, but it was demonstrated and made tangible in the armistice arrangements setting up the Russian zones in Germany, Austria, and Korea, and in the headlong rush to demobilize now that peace had been achieved.

Subsequent events revealed error in the estimates on which we acted at the close of the Second World War. Soviet Russia embarked at once upon a program of troublemaking and aggression, infiltrating border states and fomenting revolution, becoming a perpetual obstructionist in the United Nations, a constant threat to our position in the joint occupation in Berlin, and the ill-concealed backer of the hostilities in Korea. Furthermore, in the postwar era Communist Russia emerged not merely as the prime menace to America and the Free World but as the only serious threat to world peace.

Throughout all our earlier experiences as a nation we had been sheltered not only by the Atlantic but by a fairly even balance of power in Europe. Napoleonic France was checked by a ring of opponents, Bismarck's Germany by rival neighbors, the Kaiser by a watchful Britain and France, and Hitler and Mussolini by a group of powers which until the actual outbreak of hostilities seemed to have the upper hand in resources and armaments. But against Russia in the postwar era there could be no effective check unless we took the lead and made the chief contribution.

Another peculiarity of the present crisis has had almost no notice. Except at the time of the French Revolution—and then the effect was blurred by the countervailing menace from England—the dangers to the United States from without have been consistently from powers that could be identified with reaction. They were from governments working in the interest of a privileged few and not, as is the profession of our system, dedicated to the general welfare. The responsive note that any of these external foes might strike within the United States therefore was strictly limited. The Barbary pirates, England of the impressments, imperial Germany with its goose-stepping militarism, and the Fascist dictators with their frank programs of rule by and for a self-proclaimed elite had little appeal to the ordinary American and nothing to offer the underprivileged or less fortunate.

Today's overarching threat from without, Soviet Russia, appears to be as totalitarian and as demoniac as the German,

Italian, and Japanese Fascists were. In theory, however, Communism is actuated by a concern for improving the lot of the common man. Unlike Naziism it professes to be no disrespecter of persons but instead to have as its prime purpose the lifting of the downtrodden and the relief of those who are oppressed. Particularly if the pure theory rather than the Russian practice could be communicated to America, there rises the specter that those who toil, those who are overtaxed and underbenefited, those who are victims of discrimination, might conceivably unite under this alien banner and overthrow the present government and society.

The fear seems unconscionably farfetched, but it is readily exploitable. For the first time within the memory of man the political philosophy farthest to the left has the same label as the external menace that everyone identifies as the most serious. Almost automatically, then, the Communist philosophy and those in America who espouse it are typed as un-American and by insinuation as unpatriotic and treasonable.

Furthermore, with minimum care to avoid precise definition of Communism or Communist, the discredit can be spread over the entire left—over Socialists, New Dealers, and liberals in general as well as out-and-out Communists. By easy extension the taint can also be communicated to every form of nonconformity, dissent, advocacy of change, or entrance into the elastic boundaries of what is called controversial. This is the circumstance that explains how the taunt of Communist could be hurled at a great miscellany of persons, groups, and causes. The complete roll call would go as high as Nobel Prize winner George Marshall and the Ford Foundation. It would include the equally preposterous charge that proposals to fluoridize drinking water were plots to soften resistance to Communism.

By the summer of 1953 the mere epithet was not enough, and informal debate had been joined on whether this group or that was "the most Communist." Senator McCarthy's aide said it was the Protestant clergy. A well-intentioned refutation, telecast to the nation, held that on its face this was in error. It claimed that everyone knew the center of Communist strength was in union labor. This idea was by no means new, calumny though it is against the vast majority of the nation's workers. Indeed, the severity of the Taft-Hartley Act is direct evidence of the hold this thought had gained.

To point at the schools and colleges as hotbeds of Communism has been almost as fashionable. Sometimes the finger has been put on Professor X or Scientist Y or Kindergarten Teacher Z. More often the charge is a broadside or an attack by unguided missile. Thus, the sponsors of progressive education have been dubbed Bolshevik. By this token it would seem that anyone who spoke up for the old-time education would be perfectly safe. But at the University of Nevada a professor was fired for circulating an article which did exactly that. One of the reactions of the Nevada regents was to require every member of the faculty to disavow Communism.

For a time the House Commmittee on Un-American Activities behaved as though the motion-picture industry was the queen cell of the Communists in America. McCarthy first achieved the limelight with wholesale charges against the State Department. From time to time after that his attention shifted to the Government Printing Office, Fort Monmouth, Harvard University, the press, the plants to which government contracts have been awarded, libraries at home and abroad, and the personnel of gas and electric companies.

The attack has gone repeatedly against writers, publishers, artists, columnists, commentators, and members of the professions. Presumably they get this attention because they are in position to influence thought. The accusation of Communism, at any rate, has been a mainstay of the anti-intellectuals. Advocates of social justice have always had a thorny path, because the comfortable could always call them trouble makers rather than trouble solvers. Nowadays they too are called Reds. It has happened also to advocates of fair-employment legislation, to exponents of minority rights, to critics of police brutality, and to foes of segregation in the armed services, in schools and churches, or in residential areas. Price and rent control, the excess profits tax, social security, required vaccination of dogs against rabies, compulsory pasteurization of milk—these and other public welfare measures have been castigated as Communist.

Similarly, the charge of Communism has been leveled at many projects for social betterment through public ownership. An alternative phrase, "Creeping Socialism," technically not identical with Communism but in the parlance of the day having much the same effect, has been bandied about in the political campaigns. Random examples of the invoking of this phrase include the fight to do away with public housing projects, the objections to federal contributions toward the school lunch program, the drive against the Rural Electrification Authority, and President Eisenhower's expressed disapproval of TVA.

International co-operation likewise falls under attack. The advocates of world federalism are accused of being un-American. The United Nations, though indorsed by both major parties and a main reliance in the foreign policy of Eisenhower and Dulles no less than in that of Truman and Acheson, is blasted as a tool of the Communists. When UNESCO is attacked, as in the push to eradicate its study in the Houston and Los Angeles schools, it is in the guise of anti-Communism. Apparently it matters not that Russia scorned UNESCO, works constantly to frustrate the United Nations, and takes no stock in world federalism.

In this variegated fashion the umbrella of anti-Communism has been unlimbered to cover a multitude of thrusts and jibes. The offhand impression may be that the charges are utterly miscellaneous; yet significant patterns do exist. The persons and movements attacked in almost all instances have proposed some change from the conventional, some step, bold or mild, toward improving the lot of the underprivileged, or some shift in the favors of government. They have the appearance thus of posing a threat to the status quo or, more accurately, to the present possessors of advantage. Name-calling, no doubt, is frequently a matter of pure emotion. It is clear, however, that the cry of

Communist is most often hurled at those who are seen as threats to the special interests.

To identify the participants in the present orgy of Communist-baiting is much more difficult. Those smeared have the tar sticking to them and are readily identifiable. Those wielding the brush do not always let themselves be seen. The poison pen letter characteristically is not signed. When the switchboard lights up with telephoned vilifications of a broadcaster, the voices do not usually identify themselves. The whispering campaign is anonymous. The FBI protects its sources, and, in "loyalty and security" procedures generally, the accusations float above any identifiable accuser.

To identify those for whom the smear is undertaken is a still more difficult question. Those out in the forefront—the noisiest congressmen, the perennial harpies at public meetings, the most frenetic and vituperative of the broadcasters—do not impress as the real power behind the campaign. On the other hand there is no logic in rushing to the conclusion that every big businessman, every political conservative, every isolationist, every person who would turn back the calendar on reclamation, conservation, public power, social security, and the like, backs the unrestrained and indiscriminate defaming that goes under the guise of anti-Communism. Powerful, wily, and ruthless backing, however, it certainly has.

To discover why the drive has been conducted is even more difficult. Certain observations, however, can be advanced with a fair degree of confidence. The most obvious is that anti-Communism rests on an element of truth. One such fact is the menace and mendacity of Russia, the home office and the copyright holder of Communism. Another is the existence of American Communists.

These Communists, it should be noted, were not distributed evenly through our society. Few or none emerged as bank presidents, captains of industry, merchant princes, or corporation lawyers. Their more frequent incidence was in the lower economic and social echelons and among persons more sensitive to the defects in the working of our system. Communist recruitment and influence were greatest on the relief rolls, in organizations striving to improve the status of the worker, in the religious groups most conscious of a social responsibility, among young students optimistically searching for new and better solutions, and among those of their elders who were most ready to consider projects for reforming our society.

It is also true that in such groups Communists often managed to gain influence out of proportion to their numbers. Whether or not they were subversive of American institutions, they certainly were disruptive of American liberalism. As examples of skilful manipulation of group dynamics their feats perhaps should excite our admiration. The almost universal reaction, however, is to resent the methods that thwarted democratic decision and enabled a few Communists to control. Similarly we register alarm at the dedication to the cause that some of these people exhibited and at the readiness often shown to shift course whenever there was a change in the party line.

On sober reflection and on inspection of the record it is impossible to maintain that every American Communist has been diabolically clever, superhumanly inspired, and constantly alert to the dictates of the Kremlin. Yet there is some actual basis for the stereotype that we have created. This stereotype, furthermore, ties in with the nature of the danger to which it is popularly believed our country is exposed. In contrast to preceding generations we are not in fear of barn-burners and bomb-throwers. We express great concern about subversives but do not seriously believe that the American Communists have any prospects of carrying off an outright revolution. Within the United States the present danger is, concretely, of espionage and, phantasmagorially, of damage being done to American morale.

Communist espionage has been certified through the detection and conviction of Fuchs, Gold, and the Rosenbergs. The Alger Hiss conviction, though on a charge of perjury, registered in the public mind as the conviction of a master spy. Without any pretense of regular trial, still other persons—Harry Dexter

White, for example—have been publicly and all but officially stigmatized as spies for Communist Russia.

Had Hiss been tried for espionage, no one can be positive what the verdict would have been. As for White, a grand jury found the evidence insufficient to warrant an indictment. In other instances where spying has been asserted, the truth has not been fully established. The hard fact remains, however, and no one can deny it, that spies were at work, and this has contributed to the hair-trigger set of the public mind with regard to spies and spying.

On the vulnerability of American morale the evidence necessarily is even less specific. To drum up anything at all impressive on this point it is necessary to hark back to the depths of the depression or to the period when Russia was our active ally. The completely unsympathetic light in which Russia now stands is enough to ruin the prospects for Communist recruitment in this country.

As a matter of fact, although the implication is always present, the professional anti-Communists have not campaigned on the basis that the United States is a sitting duck for Communism, that the American people are gullible and will be taken in by Communist propaganda. Sometimes they have advanced this view about American youth, who, they say, must be shielded against the distortions of Communist teaching. More often, the emphasis has been put on spy rings, on the preservation of our military and scientific secrets, and on the tenet that not a penny of the taxpayers' money should find its way into the hands of a Communist.

Reduced to its core, the attitude is that Communists are unclean or, in the vernacular, that they are dirt. The investigating committees regard all Communists as pariahs who should be cut off from every visible means of support. Congressman Jackson and others would withdraw from them the protection of the Fifth Amendment. President Eisenhower would go further and rescind their citizenship. Former Governor Shivers of Texas would have them executed.

37

Guarding against spies may be a reason for these proposals. Protecting the patriotism of Americans in general has the appearance of a much less genuine motive. Flat hatred of Communists just because they are Communists probably is closer to the real explanation.

Centuries ago, in the Roman Senate, Cato had the monopoly on the anti-Carthaginian slogan. With us there has been competitive shouting of *delenda est Communism*. It has echoed ever since the twenties. It was the stock in trade of the bitter foes of the New Deal. Hitler and Goebbels went into tirades against Communism and pictured the Nazi regime as the bulwark of the West against this evil force. All through the Second World War, even when Russia was doing yeoman service as our ally, a segment of Americans held to the position that Communist Russia was our greatest cause for concern. Shortly after the end of the war this opinion rapidly gained ground. It had a few principal spokesmen, of whom the most prominent came to be McCarthy, but the really significant feature was the multitude of voices denouncing Communism in general and the American Communists in particular. Editors, columnists, commentators, pundits, orators from pulpit, school platform, and every other rostrum, candidates for all offices, President Truman and President Eisenhower indistinguishably, J. Edgar Hoover in the name of the FBI, and practically everyone else who was articulate joined this chorus. Committees of Congress elaborately reported "findings" that condemned the Communist party as a conspiracy and an agency of a foreign government, while essayists and philosophers reasoned their way to the same conclusion. This barrage helped build up a popular attitude of hostility toward this peculiar minority; the hardening of public opinion stimulated the verbal onslaughts; and the whole thing snowballed.

Actions of Soviet Russia added fuel to this fire, and at the same time various incidents on the domestic front seemed to document the internal threat to security. Pressure, meanwhile, came from standing organizations such as the American Legion and from others created for the purpose such as the Minute Women.

The net result was to make the Communist the low man on the totem pole, the most despised of all Americans. Just when he gained that unenviable distinction would be hard to say, but certainly it was before McCarthy discovered him in 1950, and from that unpopularity he was not at all rescued by the rebuke and rejection that befell McCarthy late in 1954.

Whenever any sentiment gets to rolling with real momentum, the human tendency is to see it as a bandwagon and jump aboard. Anti-Communism drew many such recruits in this post-war era. It had another overpowering attraction because in practice it turned out to be a devastating bludgeon against liberalism and nonconformity. Nominally aimed at Communists, it flattened many who by any rational test could not have been thus identified, and it sent others cowering and timorously on guard lest they share the same fate. As this power came to be recognized, it added an ulterior motive. The usefulness of the weapon against a whole sector of political and social opinion became a prime reason for the rallying to the crusade against Communism. That is what has made membership on one of the investigating committees such a plum.

Whereas most political accusations have the disadvantage of being two-edged swords, as apt to cut to right as to the left, the accusation of Communism has the beauty of cutting only to the left. It works against labor but not against employers, against the radical but not against the reactionary, against reformers but not against standpatters. In non-political areas a few conservatives have been hurt—in the cruder of the "loyalty" purges, for example. But in politics proper the real damage has been confined to the Democratic party.

Because the Democrats were in power, such Communists as got into federal employment between 1933 and 1952 are held as a liability of the Democratic administrations. Over that same period the non-conspiratorial aims of the American Communists —for a better deal for labor, racial minorities, and the underprivileged—were much closer to the program of the Democrats, the party of reform, than to the intentions of the Republicans. Consequently, the gravitational pull was chiefly between Communists and Democrats. Because they were in office, the Democrats at the same time had opportunity to get in the strongest blows against the Communists abroad, where the real danger is, and to restrain Communism in America. They accomplished much on both fronts. In spite of these achievements, in current politics a charge of Communism or Communist sympathy can be counted on to damage a Democrat but not a Republican.

Thus Adlai Stevenson's chances for the Presidency were hurt because, when interrogated by the court, he had done his duty as a citizen and a member of the bar by certifying that Hiss's reputation had been good, which was true. President Eisenhower and Secretary of State Dulles, on the contrary, are unsullied by having retained Hiss as head of the Carnegie Corporation long after charges against him had been lodged. Candidates Case in New Jersey and Javits in New York had to deny or explain away certain charges, but the smear did not work against them. And it matters not that the Communists in Wisconsin supported McCarthy in his first candidacy for the Senate. The Democrats have just about learned that on this issue "you-too-ism" does not work. Which is just as well. But there is left in the Republican arsenal a weapon that the Democrats do not possess.

The explanations for the virulence of anti-Communism as a domestic issue thus are complicated. They contain a mixture of fact and distortion. Chief among them may be the political hay that can be made. In a way, however, this is a superficial view of the matter. No hue and cry can be effective unless ears are trained and hearers conditioned to respond. The ground for most serious concern is that the American people got into the habit of responding automatically to the shout of Communist without so much as asking for any other evidence or, indeed, for any evidence.

4. The Inquisitors

The drive against Communists in America has been too complex to be assigned to a single cause or to be symbolized by any one man. There is no question, however, that this drive is the first major movement in the United States to find its dynamics in the agency of the investigating committee. Pamphleteers like Tom Paine got much of the credit for building up sentiment for American independence in 1776. On the slavery issue the press was vocal, but the limelight went to the abolitionists and the Lincoln-Douglas debates. The oratory of Bryan lifted the silver question to its peak. The lurid journalism of the muckrakers touched off the reform drives of the early years of this century. The New Deal was personified in Franklin Delano Roosevelt and communicated through his fireside chats.

For the postwar and domestic phases of anti-Communism and the particular way in which it has been prosecuted the labels commonly used point straight to the investigating committees. First it was the gospel according to Martin Dies. Later J. Parnell Thomas was the apostle. Local phases put the stress on such names as Tenney in California, Broyles in Illinois, and Ober in Maryland, and nationally sometimes on Velde or Jenner or Brownell, but much more often, and deservedly so, we have called it McCarthyism. These labels bring to mind much that goes beyond the pure work of investigation. That, however, is the upright to which they are attached.

In order to arm themselves with the facts, our legislative bodies have used the technique of investigation almost from the beginning. Sometimes it was by the same standing committees that had responsibility for drafting or appraising certain types of proposed legislation. At other times it was by a special committee created for the task of gathering the facts on a specific problem. As the Congress and some of the legislatures got larger and more unwieldy, and as the problems of government grew more complex, the need for systematic fact-gathering increased. Also, the assignment of added authority to the administration made it advisable to set up committees to keep check on the actual operations of the executive branch. Usually these committees have been narrowed to a limited field, but their character is investigatory.

In these various shapes—the regular, the watchdog, and the special—committees of the Congress and the legislature have piled up a long history of this kind of work. Some of its chapters are highly honorable. A few examples will illustrate.

Throughout the decades following the Civil War there was much talk about the power of Wall Street and the monopolization of American banking. It remained, however, for the Pujo committee, chartered by Congress in 1911, to document the assertion that there was a "money trust." After careful investigation this committee reported that such a combination did exist, with J. P. Morgan at its apex and with interlocking directorates as the most favored technique. The Federal Reserve Act of 1913 was a direct outgrowth of this report.

In the twenties fingers of suspicion were pointed at several henchmen of President Harding. Attorney-General Daugherty made only the most perfunctory motions toward prosecution. There, or approximately there, the matter might have rested except that Senator Thomas J. Walsh of Montana went ahead with a thorough investigation which revealed unpleasant facts about manipulation of the Navy's oil reserves at Teapot Dome and Elk Hills. Thus prodded, the Coolidge administration had to act, and as a result there were resignations, indictments, prosecutions, and convictions.

Another less famous example of vigorous and wholesome fact-gathering is the work of the Tolan committee in its investigation of the treatment of migratory labor in California agriculture. Carey McWilliams and others had written documented exposés. John Steinbeck had dramatized the plea in his *Grapes of Wrath*. The plight of the workers was widely known; yet local government apparently could not be counted on for a remedy. The Tolan committee sought to establish the facts about the distress of the workers. Through vigorous, even merciless, questioning it also probed into the reasons for this distress, specifically the practices of the employers whereby these workers were victimized. Remedial action, it must be admitted, was only fragmentary.

Another committee that compiled a noteworthy record was the one the Senate set up to keep an eye on the conduct of the Second World War. Its chairman had been a run-of-the-mill senator and before that a haberdasher and a captain of artillery. It was his alert, persistent, vigorous, and scrupulous work as head of this committee that earned him the vice-presidency in 1944, out of which came the Presidency from 1945 through 1952.

A more recent example was the transcontinental investigation of organized crime conducted by the Kefauver committee. Although marred by hippodrome tactics and too much geared to television, this investigation impressed the American people as a force for decency, integrity, and improved law enforcement. It gave Senator Kefauver national stature and greatly encouraged his candidacy for the Democratic nomination for President in 1952.

These five are examples of how investigating committees can work. Unfortunately, they do not illustrate how such committees always behave.

A change amounting to a new dispensation came as recently as 1938 when the House of Representatives created its Un-

American Activities Committee with Martin Dies as chairman. The committee was given a broad and vague charge to investigate "the extent, character, and objects of un-American propaganda activities in the United States" and "the diffusion within the United States of subversive and un-American propaganda that is instigated from foreign countries or of domestic origin." Carefully worded instructions might have pointed the committee toward a fruitful career. Yet, more than its stated aim, what gave this committee its peculiar distinction was its choice and development of techniques.

As of 1938 there was only meager precedent for congressional investigation into subversion. The first instance had been in 1919. In February of that year, just a few months after the Armistice, two meetings were held in Washington to rally support for the new Bolshevik regime in Russia. Stirred by the sensational press reports on these meetings, the Senate ordered an investigation and assigned it to a Judiciary Committee subcommittee which had been set up to investigate the brewing industry. From the brewers the committee had gone on to German wartime propaganda and by that experience was thought to be qualified for this further assignment. After questioning a number of witnesses, this subcommittee filed a report which was primarily a description of the workings of the Bolshevik government in Russia. It went on to speculate on what the introduction of such a system would mean in the United States. No legislation was proposed.

The next venture into investigation of subversive activities came eleven years later, in 1930. Grover Whalen, police commissioner of New York, precipitated it by charging that the Amtorg Trading Corporation was a Communist propaganda agency. A House committee presided over by Hamilton Fish came back with a highly colored and inconsistent report. Its findings were that there was no evidence in support of the charges against Amtorg and that the Communist movement in the United States was most feeble; yet its recommendations were for drastic measures to suppress the Communist party. No such law was enacted.

Four years later, following Hitler's rise to power, the House chartered another special committee to look into "Nazi propaganda activities in the United States" and, more broadly, into "subversive propaganda that is instigated from foreign countries and attacks the principle of the form of government as guaranteed by our Constitution." Under the chairmanship of John McCormack this committee made a prompt, efficient investigation. Its findings were not sensational: neither Fascism nor Communism was making appreciable headway among Americans. One piece of legislation did result, the McCormack Act of 1938, requiring registry of foreign propaganda agents. The exemplary record of the McCormack committee undoubtedly was a factor in the decision of the House in 1938 when Dies proposed the creation of the Un-American Activities Committee.

His motion touched off a lively debate, confined by House rules to a single hour. Much was said, however, that has added interest because of the subsequent course of the committee. For one thing, although concern about Communists was expressed, the danger from Fascism, particularly Naziism, was clearly the main consideration that disposed the House to set up such a committee. J. Parnell Thomas, for one, cited a Nazi camp in his district in New Jersey. Some congressmen protested the ill-defined and unlimited authorization proposed for the committee. Gerald J. Boileau would have preferred an investigation directed to "propaganda activities in the United States which have as their object the overthrow of the Government of the United States by force and violence." His amendment fell before a parliamentary maneuver without so much as a vote.

In his remarks on the motion, Dies admitted that such a committee might do more harm than good if it fell into the hands of men intent on gaining publicity or rousing hatred against minority groups. He promised that, if he had anything to do with the committee, there would be scrupulous respect for the rights of individuals. He expressed doubt that such a committee would recommend new legislation. To try to prevent un-American activities by law, he feared, "might jeopardize fundamental rights far more important than the objective we seek." He was confident, however, that the committee could accomplish a great good by exposure of subversive activities. This debate, though not always in step with the subsequent course of the committee, was an intriguing preview.

An additional forecast on the work of the committee is contained in Dies's opening remarks at its first session. He said the committee would operate on "a dignified plane" and with "a judicial attitude." It would be "fair and impartial at all times and treat every witness with fairness and courtesy." It would "not permit any 'character assassination' or any 'smearing' of innocent people," and would be "more concerned with facts than with opinions, and with specific proof than with generalities." The committee, he promised, would not adopt "a partisan or preconceived attitude." Opinions and philosophies that we do not agree with, he reminded, are not necessarily un-American. "The utmost care, therefore, must be observed to distinguish clearly between what is obviously un-American and what is no more or less than an honest difference of opinion with respect to some economic, political, or social question."

No homily could have been more sensible or more reassuring. But, after this the deluge.

By means of periodic renewals Dies was able to parlay the initial seven-month authorization into a seven-year term as head of this committee. From an inquiry into Fascist propaganda, which at the outset was the chief justification, he promptly shifted the emphasis to Communist-hunting. With Hitler on the rampage and the Second World War in process during most of Dies's seven years, this was no mean feat. He was frank, too, in announcing another target, the New Deal, which was "un-American" because it departed from the system of free enterprise as conceived by Dies. Semantics, it must be admitted, was all on Dies's side. "Communist" all along grated on American ears, whereas "free enterprise" had a hallowed sound.

It was on method, fully as much as on name, that the Dies committee thrived. The beginning was with committee hearings at which witnesses were called upon to describe Communist activities in the United States and to name participants. Through allegations by witnesses, these named persons were identified as members or participants in various organizations such as groups for social betterment, slum clearance, equal rights, better schools, and relief of refugees from Fascism, of Spanish war orphans, and of American dust bowl victims.

With even a meager basis of testimony, the staff of the Dies committee now could spread a wide net. It went down the roster of organizations in which known or asserted Communists appeared, ticking off the names. Similarly it combed lists of sponsors of relief drives, banquets, lecture series, and the like. Names thus acquired were then applied as the communicant of taint to other groups. No careful distinction was made between direct association with an alleged Communist and what might be called association once or twice removed. Nor was there much attempt to weigh the amount, degree, or purpose of this associating. A reduction to absurdity besets this device, as is illustrated by the linkage of such pillars of respectability as Governors Elmer A. Benson of Minnesota, Frank Murphy of Michigan, and Culbert Olson of California. The fallacy, however, is as great and the damage more serious in the involvement of a multitude of persons less well known but equally loyal. Theoretically the door was open for them to come to the committee and deny any false allegations. The thing that really needed to be demolished was the notion that such associations spelled guilt.

In 1948 the number of names in the files of the committee was said by its chief investigator to be a million, and every single one of them stigmatized as having been in some degree un-American. Potentially this was a mammoth stockpile for blackmail and blacklisting. Particularly in the hands of a congressional committee it could be an influence on employment practices and perhaps even on policy-making in the executive branch of the government.

The other kingpin in the method of Dies and his committee was an insatiate grasping for publicity. Dies was working in the dark days before television. Radio time was seldom if ever directly available. But the press was his best friend. He mastered the knack of making headlines. A charge made by a current witness might do the trick, or Dies's comment on the day's hearing, and there were always the files from which some morsel could be plucked. Dies exhibited a genius too for commandeering any issue that caught public interest. Again and again he moved in ahead of other congressional committees where their concern would have been more legitimate. On this score the Dies committee has been likened to a neurotic watchdog barking furiously at every passer-by.

Superficially, it appears that barking was all the committee did. In the Dies era the only piece of legislation proposed was a rider to the Treasury–Post Office appropriation bill in 1943, to forbid payments to thirty-nine employees whom Dies branded as "irresponsible, unrepresentative, crackpot radical bureaucrats" and participants in Communist-front organizations. After hearings, a House subcommittee pared the list to three, Robert M. Lovett, Goodwin Watson, and William E. Dodd, Jr. The House enacted the bill with such a rider. Impelled by the necessity of meeting Post Office payrolls, the Senate reluctantly concurred, and President Roosevelt still more reluctantly withheld veto. Taken to court, the rider was easily identified as a bill of attainder, a punishment of named individuals without a judicial trial. The trial court so recognized it and the Supreme Court held the rider unconstitutional. As Justice Black's opinion reminded, "When our Constitution and Bill of Rights were written, our ancestors had ample reason to know that legislative trials and punishments were too dangerous to liberty to exist in the nation of free men they envisaged."

When the Seventy-ninth Congress assembled in 1945, the likelihood seemed to be that the Committee on Un-American Activities would be allowed to lapse. The committee as such had gone practically dormant, and Chairman Dies, though still much in the headlines, had not sought re-election to Congress. It was John Rankin of Mississippi, long a stalwart supporter of the Dies interpretation of Americanism, who came to the rescue. An ostensible motive was to guarantee preservation of the Dies committee files. On the first day of the new Congress, when the customary motion was made to retain in effect the rules of the preceding Congress, Rankin offered an amendment to add the Un-American Activities Committee as a standing committee. Until the motion was passed there was no Rules Committee to which the proposal might be referred. Therefore, it had to be voted on by the House. A majority probably did not want such a committee, but to vote against investigation of un-American activities was thought to be most hazardous politically. A coalition of Republican and southern Democratic votes carried the amendment, 207 to 186.

In 1945 and 1946 the committee's work was inconsequential. An inquiry into the publicity efforts of the Office of Price Administration proved abortive. Later the committee interrogated such witnesses as Earl Browder, William Z. Foster, Gerald L. K. Smith, and Louis F. Budenz, but to no particular profit.

In the hands of the Republicans of the Eightieth Congress— J. Parnell Thomas, Earl Mundt, and Richard Nixon, in particular—the committee was transformed into a much more vigorous and sensational agency. On assuming the chairmanship, Thomas announced a program of ferreting out Communists and Communist sympathizers in the government; exposing Communist influence in labor, atomic bomb projects, Hollywood, and education; providing a reference service on subversive and un-American activities for the use of Congress and the investigating units of the government and the armed services; and carrying to the American people counterpropaganda against subversives. There is serious question whether this last is a proper function of the committee. It turned out to be the most emphasized of all.

The revitalized committee began with a questioning of asserted "functionaries" in the Communist party. Since some were aliens, the inquiry became a vehicle for challenging the

State Department for its practices in admitting refugees from Fascist oppression. An inquiry into Communist infiltration of unions turned up little that was new. The committee then held hearings on two loosely drawn bills that in effect would have outlawed the Communist party. One, authored by Rankin, had a provision making a teacher liable to a fine of $10,000 and imprisonment for ten years if he should "convey the impression of sympathy with . . . Communist ideology." Witnesses such as William C. Bullitt, William Green, Eric Johnston, and J. Edgar Hoover counseled against these measures. The witnesses in favor were much less impressive. One Walter S. Steele, who identified himself as head of a sort of holding company for American patriotic and fraternal groups, held forth at length, indiscriminately denouncing literally hundreds of organizations and thousands of persons for subversive activities. When he was through, Chairman Thomas thanked him profusely, saying that in his eight years on the committee he had never seen "a more complete and more documented statement."

Later in the year the committee opened its greatest publicity gold mine with an inquiry into Communism in American movie-making. The Dies committee had made gestures in this direction and Rankin had made broad charges, but the full-dress performance was left for 1947. In May a subcommittee went to California and in executive session heard a dozen "friendly" witnesses, including Jack Warner, Robert Taylor, and Adolph Menjou. Their testimony was never made public but, ostensibly on the basis of it, Thomas gave out the subcommittee report. It asserted that scores of screen writers were Communists, that they had injected Communist propaganda into movies, that much of this had been very subtle, but that the committee "had a list" of all such pictures produced in the last eight years. It further asserted that a number of loyal actors and directors had refused to have a part in making Communist-tinged pictures and that the Communists had prevented the making of other pictures that would have glorified America and the American system. Publicity-wise this was a come-on for the October presentation.

Opening these hearings, Thomas announced that evidence would be unfolded to prove: (1) that Communists had infiltrated the picture industry, especially the Screen Writers Guild, (2) that Communist propaganda had been put into particular movies, and (3) that the White House had pressured the industry to produce pro-Soviet films.

The friendly witnesses were heard first. Their testimony turned out to be considerably less explicit than Thomas had forecast. Warner insisted that *Mission to Moscow*, made in 1942, was intended to aid the war effort and that it was true to Ambassador Davies' book. When asked to evaluate the picture in terms of the international situation of 1947, he countered, "How did I, or you, or anyone else know in 1942 what the conditions were going to be in 1947?"

As to *Song of Russia*, also of the vintage of 1942, Louis B. Mayer was equally emphatic that of course it was friendly to Russia, then our ally. He could not, however, see it as a propaganda piece. It was, he said, just a pleasant romance, set in Russia to justify bringing in Tschaikovsky's music.

The committee counsel tried to bring out evidence of Communist propaganda in other pictures—Mrs. Lela E. Rogers, for example, professed to see it in *None but the Lonely Heart*—but the charges seemed specious throughout. The promised exposure of Communist-infected films did not come off.

As to White House or government pressure for pro-Russian releases, some of the assertions presumably made in the California hearings dissolved into thin air. Warner now denied that Davies had suggested the filming of *Mission to Moscow* and insisted that it was the studio that had made the approach. And Robert Taylor, who according to Thomas had been forced by government officials to do *Song of Russia* before being allowed to enter the Navy, now stoutly denied that any such thing had happened. The committee found no corroboration for its charge of pressure from the White House.

In the second week of its sessions on the picture industry the committee turned to the matter of identifying Communist members and affiliates. The procedure was to put a witness on the stand and ask, "Are you now or have you ever been a member of the Communist party in the United States?" Ten of the first eleven witnesses called proved to be "unfriendly." The first of these was John Howard Lawson. He asked permission to read an introductory statement and was refused. When asked whether he had been a member of the Screen Writers Guild, he parried by challenging the authority of the committee to ask such a question. Similarly, to the question about Communist party membership, he objected that it was an invasion of his rights. He alluded to the Bill of Rights but did not precisely ground his refusal to answer on the Fifth or any other amendment.

After a heated exchange of words, which did not include a direct answer to the question, Lawson was removed from the stand. In his place came a committee investigator who put into the record an elaborate dossier on Lawson's activities and associations. The most concrete assertion was that Lawson's Communist party "registration card" for 1944 bore the number 47275. The impression conveyed was that this proved membership, though in *The Time of the Toad* Dalton Trumbo later argued that it was no more than "the alleged office record of an alleged card." From this level the revelations trailed off to such subjective assertions as that Lawson had hailed "the rise of the revolutionary theater."

The same routine held for nine other "unfriendly" witnesses. They came to the stand, sharply exchanged unpleasantries with the committee and its counsel, and, having refused to answer personal and political questions, were replaced by the committee's investigator with the appropriate dossier from the committee files. After each such performance the committee members voted unanimously that the witness be cited for contempt.

After four days of such work, Chairman Thomas totted up the score as eleven of Hollywood's most prominent Communist suspects heard from and sixty-eight to go. Then, for reasons not altogether clear, he abruptly adjourned the hearings. A possible explanation is that, in spite of lavish space given the hearings, the press was beginning to point up the ludicrousness of the committee's work. Obsession with the question on Communist membership kept the committee from any serious effort at drawing out information from the witnesses. The committee did not show a genuine concern for fact-finding. Nor did it prepare a formal report of its findings. Its substitute was the contempt proceedings against the Hollywood Ten.

In the summer of 1948, with a national election approaching, the committee moved into an investigation of Communist espionage. A Senate subcommittee led the way when it drew in Elizabeth Bentley as a witness, and she told of channeling secret documents from federal employees to the Russians. Furthermore, a federal grand jury in New York, which under the Smith Act had indicted a dozen officers of the Communist party, was rumored to have a lead on Communists in federal employ. Never voluntarily in the back seat when it came to the search for Communists, the Un-American Activities Committee rushed in, somewhat to the handicap of the grand jury and its work.

What unfolded is a well-known story. It began with testimony from two former Communists who admitted having been spy-couriers, Miss Bentley and Whittaker Chambers. The stories that they told came forth piecemeal, seemingly with some parts deliberately held back, and each in part self-contradictory. Both named particular federal employees, some quite highly placed, who had been the source of supply for documents to forward to Russia, or who they had reason to believe were Communists or Communist agents. Some of the persons named came before the committee and categorically denied the allegations.

The committee did not follow up on all the leads provided by Bentley and Chambers. Much less did it undertake to measure and assess the degree of truth in the charges that several spy rings had functioned in the government offices. Instead, it chose to personalize the issue and to concentrate on a few individuals, notably Alger Hiss. His volunteered denial, the confrontation with Chambers, his delayed admission that he had known Chambers under another name, his challenge to Chambers to repeat the charges without benefit of immunity, the libel suit, and the two trials for perjury need not be rehearsed.

Doubts remain as to what the committee was up to at certain stages in the investigation. There is no doubt, however, that the committee had a key role in getting Hiss convicted. Its relentless interrogation produced the answers that were held to be in perjury and provoked the libel suit, which led to the indictment. The committee also produced some of the witnesses and evidence vital to the prosecution in the perjury trials. Perhaps more important was the way in which the committee contributed to the climate of opinion in which the charges against Hiss were received. Unlike the grand jury, the committee worked in and for the full glare of publicity. From day to day as the hearings progressed, committee members interpolated comments on the enormity of the abuses they were uncovering. By exaggerating his role and influence in government, the committee made Hiss the symbol of the New Deal. It was in the headlines almost daily with some comment or disclosure on Hiss until the end of the year when the grand jury returned the perjury indictment. Six months later, when the first trial ended with a hung jury, Nixon denounced the trial judge as incompetent and the Truman administration as not wanting a conviction. After January 21, 1950, with the conviction achieved, Nixon and his fellow committeemen were by no means backward about appropriating the credit.

Two other items on the agenda in 1948 exemplify the methods of the committee. One was the issuance of a "preliminary" report branding Dr. Edward U. Condon, director of the National Bureau of Standards, as "one of the weakest links in our atomic security." The report, though brief, was a tissue of misrepresentation and innuendo. Within hours the Department of Commerce announced that its loyalty board six days earlier had given Condon full clearance. Thomas issued a bellicose rejoinder. Condon repeatedly demanded a chance to defend himself before the committee. Other members of the House, notably Chet

Holifield and Helen Gahagan Douglas, came to his defense and so did practically the whole fraternity of American scientists. Perhaps because of the strength of this reaction, the committee let the matter lie. It retracted nothing and made no apology, but it did not go beyond its "preliminary" findings.

Another illustration of the propensity to indulge in personal attack came in the Laurence Duggan affair. On December 20, 1948, Duggan, who was director of the Institute of International Education, died in a fall from a window of his sixteenth-floor office in New York. The police found no evidence of violence, and family and friends were firmly convinced that it was an accident rather than suicide.

On receipt of the news, Mundt, Nixon, and Counsel Stripling made a midnight rush to the Un-American Activities Committee files and, after checking in them, released to the press a statement that Duggan, a friend of Hiss, had been named by Chambers as one of six who had passed confidential information to him for transmission to the Communists.

To the press the next day Chambers denied that he had said Duggan turned over any papers to him. Attorney-General Tom Clark announced that investigations made by the FBI had uncovered no evidence that Duggan was linked with espionage or with the Communist party, but on the contrary that he was a loyal employee. From their colleagues and from the press, Mundt and Nixon drew blunt criticism for their trigger-happy headline hunting. They were semiapologetic. What had been done, however, was hardly more than an intensification of what had come to be the customary tone of the committee's procedure.

With the Eighty-first Congress, 1949–50, the committee reverted to Democratic chairmanship and majority. Its behavior was much more restrained, one index being that questioning was left in much greater degree to the staff members. Some of the subjects investigated had a high potential for public interest—for example, that of asserted Communist cells in the atomic projects. Yet the headlines were not so numerous and not so big. One good reason was that the committee was coasting along in the wake of the FBI and perhaps the armed services investigations. What it was doing—and the FBI may have wanted it that way—was to put on public record a list of names, together with testimony about them, that already had been placed in the FBI files. The typical witness now was a former FBI man. Through 1951 and 1952 this pattern continued with even greater emphasis on putting names, names, names on record.

Improved though the conduct of the committee was, there was still room for criticism. Testimony taken in executive session, and perhaps on that account less restrained than it otherwise would have been, was sometimes made public. In a hearing granted Hazel Scott Powell so that she might deny charges made against her, the discussion veered to *Counterattack* and *Red Channels* in which Mrs. Powell protested she had been misused. From the California Committee on Un-American Activities, these sheets had picked up false charges against her. Representative Harrison would hear no complaint against these private publications. They had the right, he said, to extract from public records. With complete disregard for logic he went on to insist that, even though the public record might be false, the private publication which copied it was not false. "They are true if they correctly quote the source."

Another episode in which the committee appeared in a bad light was in its badgering of Max Lowenthal. A lawyer with a long and distinguished record in public service, he was haled before the committee and subjected to sharp and antagonistic questioning. What piqued the committee presumably was that Lowenthal had written a book about the FBI in which he had dared to voice some criticisms of its methods and performance. In this day and age such criticism may be enough to alert the legislative investigators. It does not excuse the way in which this probe was pushed into matters quite extraneous. Guilt by association, for example, was hinted in his connection with the nonpolitical Twentieth Century Fund. To top it off, the committee published the transcript of the Lowenthal testimony under the title *Hearings Regarding Communism in the United States Government.*

Within the span of fifteen years Dies and his successors had made the Un-American Activities Committee an institution. In the definition given to "un-American" and in their patterns of procedure they had developed a highly potent instrument. The committee files bulged with names, now far into the second million, of persons cited for un-Americanism. The committee had settled down into a routine of "education" and exposure rather than the drafting of laws. It had spread the impression that its staff work was so effective that none but the guilty were subpoenaed to appear before it. An increasing number of witnesses pleaded the Fifth Amendment and committee members loudly protested this loophole. As to net results, however, it made little difference. A mere summons to appear was enough to stamp a man in the people's view as a subversive and in many lines to cost him his job, no matter what course the hearings might take.

Above all, the committee had proved itself a political asset, a means of spotlighting selected bits of the record of past administrations, an effective leverage for Congress against the executive departments, a club over the heads of possible critics of the status quo, and, through its disfavor of so many organizations, a curb on efforts at social and political reform.

Inevitably the committee inspired imitators. In Illinois the Broyles commission ran a parallel course. The state of Washington had its Canwell committee engaged in a Dies-like hunt for subversives. Its excesses brought it into disfavor and the state legislature let it lapse. In California the Tenney committee applied the Dies formula, with emphasis on holding individuals up to discredit. In 1949 the legislature rebuffed Tenney by closing down his Senate committee. In its place arose a committee of the legislature with Senator Hugh M. Burns as chairman. Its work was less flamboyant, but like the more recent congressional investigations, its power and influence in many respects came to be greater than Tenney's ever were.

Imitation spread further. The Feinberg Act in New York has the effect of giving the state school authorities investigatory or inquisitorial authority resembling that of an un-American activities committee and with direct power of enforcement. In California the Luckel Act of 1953 confers such powers on the State Board of Education, and the Dilworth Act does the same for every local school board. Other state and local governing bodies and an untold number of non-governmental agencies have also entered the hunt for subversives, using approximate facsimiles of this same technique. In 1953, for example, the American Council of Education proposed establishment of a "central educational investigation service," which in co-operation with the FBI would enable educational institutions to do their own "housecleaning of subversives."

Another extension of this investigatory impulse is illustrated by the Norwalk Plan. As early as 1950, J. Edgar Hoover asked the public to help the FBI by reporting to it any indication of subversiveness observed in neighbors and acquaintances. Informants, it was promised, would not be identified. Four years later the Norwalk, Connecticut, post of the Veterans of Foreign Wars disclosed that it had made this a group project, acting as a clearinghouse and preliminary investigating agency on subversives among their fellow townsmen. The nationwide reaction was mixed, but it seemed to indicate that organized accusation under the immunity of secrecy was widespread and almost commonplace.

A more direct testimonial to the prowess of the committee as the great accuser was the appearance of parasitic organizations. Several have flourished, "performing a public service" by collating the passages in the testimony before the committee where a charge of un-Americanism had been lodged against a particular person. The proprietors of *Counterattack, Red Channels, Reducators,* and *Alert* claim special expertness in detecting and measuring the evidence on subversiveness. At the same time they have managed thus far to cloak themselves in the immunity of the committees, whose reports they claim to be quoting rather than interpreting.

In the light of the flimsy, immaterial, contradictory, prejudiced, and unverified character of so much of the testimony presented to the Dies committee, its successor, and its imitators, it is fantastic that unevaluated extracts therefrom should carry weight. Yet that has seemed to be the result. In pictures, radio, and television, the persons whose records are recapitulated in the parasitic sheets were very likely to be unemployable. In other avenues of employment the ax has fallen less dramatically, but the signs are that it has fallen. Members of the committee have vacillated between claiming and disowning such results. Clearly these consequences represent the lengthened arm of the committee. In the eloquent words of Adlai Stevenson:

Disturbing things have taken place in our own land. The pillorying of the innocent has caused the wise to stammer and the timid to retreat. I would shudder for this country if I thought that we too must surrender to the sinister figure of the Inquisitor, of the great accuser. I hope that the time will never come in America when charges are taken as the equivalent of facts, when suspicions are confused with certainties, and when the voice of the accuser stills every other voice in the land.

The example of the Dies committee and its successor was not lost on Congress. The same definition of un-American, the same stress on publicity as excuse for propagandizing the American people, the same irresponsibility in accusations, the same zeal to expose suspects and to condemn them without trial, the same determination to make this form of patriotism yield personal and partisan advantage were soon exhibited by other congressmen and other committees. For example, Representative Clare Hoffman of the Government Operations Committee staged one-man hearings in Detroit and Los Angeles, well timed to influence the outcome, respectively, of a strike and a local election. Similarly, in its inquest on United States policy in Asia, the McCarran committee of the Senate emulated the methods of the Un-American Activities Committee down to the characteristic determination to pillory particular individuals. It was the hearings of this committee that provided the technicalities on which Owen Lattimore was prosecuted.

An even more apt pupil was Senator McCarthy of Wisconsin. At first he did not have the advantage of membership on an investigating committee and had to pose more as a tribune for the people, decrying the presence of Communist members and sympathizers and denouncing assorted officeholders for apathy or softness toward such un-Americans. He played the role so vigorously that before long his name had become a byword for this species of patriotic demagoguery.

With Dies in the background and McCarthyism in the foreground, the Republican campaign slogans of 1952, that it was "time for a change" and that "the mess" in Washington must be cleaned up, had a special significance. The signs were that inquisitorial and accusatory tactics would be stepped up, as indeed they were when the new administration took over in 1953.

The legitimate descendant of the Dies committee, the House Un-American Activities Committee, took a new lease on belligerency under Harold Velde as chairman. The mark of heredity was no less visible in the Senate committees headed by Jenner and McCarthy. It can also be detected in the public denunciations indulged in by Attorney-General Brownell. Certain new and ingenious devices were introduced, some of which drew criticism from the original holder of the patent, Martin Dies, once again a member of the House. This later manifestation that goes under the name of McCarthy is a chapter in itself. Its basis, however, is in the extension of the investigatory method as begun by Dies back in 1938. That is what started the march of the inquisitors.

5. Descent to McCarthyism

At the opening of the Eightieth Congress in 1947 one of the lesser dramas was the seating of a new senator from Wisconsin, Joseph R. McCarthy. What ambitions then stirred in his breast are not recorded, but certainly it did not occur to any observer to predict that within half a dozen years this senator would be the most powerful in America, the most feared, and, in the estimate of Senator Taft, the GOP's "biggest asset." Every columnist and commentator has tried to explain how this came about. Here the task is to measure the consequences to the freedoms.

The new senator could be regarded as in the best American tradition a self-made man. As a farm boy he got an early introduction to hard work. As a youth he built up a thriving chicken business but because of illness lost the whole investment of plowed-back profits. With various jobs he worked his way through college and law school, and for a brief period practiced law. Then at thirty, in a campaign that featured a prodigious amount of handshaking, he got himself elected circuit judge in upstate Wisconsin. On the bench McCarthy's claim to distinction was in the volume of cases handled. He kept his court open long hours, often far into the night, and reached his decisions with dispatch. Experts on the law may not have been greatly impressed, and one case, that of the Quaker Dairy, was something of a scandal, but the press on the whole complimented his work as a judge.

Shortly after the United States' entrance into the Second World War, McCarthy persuaded neighboring judges to take on the work of his circuit while he entered the Marine Corps as a first lieutenant. After stateside duty he was sent to the South Pacific. In the traditional rituals to Neptune as the transport crossed the equator he suffered his war wound, a broken ankle. His work was as intelligence officer, but he went along as observer on a number of reconnaissance flights, hence the sobriquet "Tailgunner Joe."

In 1944 McCarthy allowed his name to be entered in the race for Republican nomination for Alexander Wiley's seat in the United States Senate. He also got a thirty-day leave to return to Wisconsin just before the primary and make a whirlwind tour of the state, though theoretically restrained by the military rules against political campaigning. He did not win but he made a good showing.

That fall, 1944, he resigned his commission and returned to his Wisconsin judgeship. His concentration, however, was on winning the Senate seat for which "young Bob" La Follette would be seeking re-election in 1946. By artful persuasion he got the indorsement of the Republican convention. He had the staunch support of the Young Republicans. He capitalized on his service record and on Republican resentment that La Follette, now returning to the fold, proposed to take charge of the party. Personal appearances all over the state, personal handwritten postcards (in many hands), and a studious generalizing on all issues were the main features of the McCarthy campaign. He won out over La Follette in the primary, apparently aided by a good many Democrats who crossed over in the "free primary" to vote for the man who looked like the weaker of the Republican candidates. There is reason to believe, too, that labor leaders later exposed as Communists put their weight against La Follette because of his all-out attacks on Communism.

In Wisconsin, Republican nomination was tantamount to election, especially in 1946 when the Roosevelt-Truman administrations were at a low ebb of popularity. McCarthy, however, left nothing to chance. Against his professorial opponent, Howard McMurray, he made the most of his own farm-boy simplicity, denouncing McMurray, meanwhile, as "Communistically" inclined. In terms of logical discussion of issues, McMurray put on much the better performance, but in backslapping, barnstorming, and getting his name to the attention of the voters, McCarthy was far ahead.

The most serious roadblock in his way was a provision in the state constitution that no circuit court judge could run for political office and that if one did the votes should not count. A taxpayer's petition to invalidate McCarthy's candidacy was taken to the Wisconsin Supreme Court, but the court in a remarkable example of casuistry referred the issue to Providence which might remove McCarthy before the election or to the voters who might defeat his candidacy at the polls. On a later motion to disbar McCarthy for having violated the lawyers' code of ethics in running despite this constitutional ban, the court was equally ingenious in refusing to set any penalty for the violation. By that time the voters of Wisconsin in ratio of almost two to one had expressed preference for McCarthy over McMurray. Before such a force, the law has often given way.

McCarthy came to the Senate a practiced politician, a rough-and-tumble campaigner, with a demonstrated capacity for hard work. The principles for which he stood were much harder to fathom, perhaps because the issues on which he had campaigned had been left so vague. In actuality he was an opportunist. And to a degree uncommon even among self-made men, he had concentrated on self-advancement. McCarthy's actions in his first three years in the Senate made his personality better known but did not reveal much about his political philosophy or program.

He took up the cudgels for a miscellaneous assortment of issues: against sugar-rationing, especially for manufacturers; against public housing projects; against the carrying-out of the sentences imposed on the Nazi perpetrators of the Malmédy massacre; and against the Department of the Navy for alleged slighting of the Marine Corps. On their face, some of these stands should have been hard to popularize in the United States. As to the amount of sugar available, it was made absolutely clear to the Senate that the facts were not as McCarthy represented; yet he had his way with an early end to rationing. At the inquiry into the war-crimes trials, he was not a member of the committee but volunteered his attendance. Throughout he was violently critical of the court, the prosecution, and the witnesses for the prosecution. His pyrotechnics did not convince the committee, which found the verdicts of the court altogether justified. Yet broadcast as they were by the press, his wild charges so inflamed public sentiment in Germany that execution of the sentences became politically impossible.

Thus far, the causes he had selected were bizarre. Fellow senators, however, were already learning to be wary of McCarthy because of his bluster, his tirades, his skill at parrying with irrelevancies, his apparent insensitivity to personal attack, and his lack of inhibitions about blasting the character of anyone who opposed him. Half of his first term was gone before McCarthy discovered the Communist issue. The day of decision is said to have been January 7, 1950, when Father Edmund Walsh of Georgetown University made the suggestion. The beginning of the new career can be pinpointed at February 9, 1950, in Wheeling, West Virginia, when with flourishes McCarthy announced that he had a list of 205 names "made known to the Secretary of State as being members of the Communist Party and who nevertheless are still working and shaping policy in the State Department."

At any time such an announcement would have been sensational. On the heels of the Hiss conviction it was especially so, and good for front-page headlines all across the continent. At Denver the next day McCarthy varied the wording but repeated the charge. At Salt Lake City on the third day he held forth in the same vein, unaccountably lowering the tally to "57 card-carrying Communists." Later he used the number 81.

Although senators have a good deal of leeway, they are subject to one control: their colleagues can call them to account. On February 20, the Senate assembled to hear McCarthy expand and itemize his Wheeling revelation. Every senator and almost every American had read McCarthy's phrase about 205 known Communist party members in the State Department. As he now quoted himself, however, the words came out, "I have in my hand 57 cases of individuals who would appear to be either card-carrying members or certainly loyal to the Communist Party, but who nevertheless are still helping to shape our foreign policy."

In at least four particulars this was a backing-down from his original assertion. As now stated, the individuals were not necessarily in the State Department. The phrase "individuals who would appear to be" qualified and weakened the charge of Communism. As now stated, they were "either card-carrying members" or something less. And the 205 had shrunk to 57. The first three discrepancies were allowed to pass, but several senators pounced on the switch in numbers. McCarthy would not meet the question head-on. He evaded it by pretending to answer, pretending then that he had answered, and insisting on going on with what he had to say. On the question of 205 or 57 the Senate got only doubletalk.

In a performance that lasted six hours McCarthy then went on to describe the "cases." Not a name was mentioned; indeed, the evidence suggests that he had no names but merely selective digests of unfavorable data collected in State Department screenings in 1946 and 1947 and later deposited in the Library of Congress. Careful analysis of what McCarthy said would have revealed that some of these individuals referred to had never been in the State Department. Others were no longer there. Still others were morals suspects but under no suspicion as Communists. Several were on the list merely because a suspected Communist had recommended them for government employment, and at least one was included on the paradoxical ground that he had been highly recommended by several sponsors "as a high type of man, a democratic American who . . . opposed Communism." Senators Lucas, McMahon, Lehman, and others tried at times to pin McCarthy down to better logic and procedure. Senators Brewster and Mundt entered occasionally with diversionary moves in his favor. The end result was no more light, but a great deal more publicity for McCarthy the anti-Communist.

Foiled in this effort to learn what tangible evidence McCarthy had, the Senate appointed a subcommittee, with Millard Tydings as chairman, to try to get McCarthy on record more specifically and more responsibly. McCarthy had proclaimed his perfect readiness to be open and frank with no hiding behind immunity. On the stand, however, he proved a most unco-operative witness. He spent a day and a half denouncing Judge Dorothy Kenyon, never a State Department employee. When Tydings pressed him to come to the point with names of State Department personnel, he pleaded for more time. Given a continuance until March 13, he finally was pushed into a corner where it seemed that he would have to name his Communists or back down with complete loss of face.

For such a predicament McCarthy had a standard maneuver. It was to veer off in another direction with a new or renewed or varied charge that would give him the advantage of the offensive again. So, on March 13, he came out with four names: an employee in the Point Four program; one in the State Department UNESCO Relations Staff; her husband, a civilian employee of the Navy; and Professor Owen Lattimore of Johns Hopkins University. As to State Department employment, McCarthy was no more than half right about these four. He was careful also to water down his charges against them almost to the point of being meaningless. They were, he said, "pro-Communists," an uncomplimentary phrase, but short of being actionable.

The next day he was back with the names of four more "pro-Communists": John Stewart Service, consular officer in Calcutta; a man who had transferred four years earlier from the State Department to the United Nations; a Harvard astronomer well out of the orbit of the State Department; and a Williams College professor who had once given a free lecture at the invitation of the State Department. This time McCarthy's range finder on the State Department was no more than a quarter right.

Granted a continuance to March 20, McCarthy again failed to produce his list of 205 known State Department Communists. Instead he elected to narrow it all down to one man and to let his charges be symbolized by that one case of Owen Lattimore, "the top Russian spy." Alerted in faraway Afghanistan, Lattimore branded the charges as "'pure moonshine'" and "'unmitigated lies." Reporters, meanwhile, were mystified to find that there was no record of his ever having been a regular employee of the State Department. Thereupon, McCarthy wavered off to the assertion that, nonetheless, he was "the chief architect of our Far Eastern policy."

The Tydings committee looked into the matter with care. The proof, McCarthy had said, was all in the FBI files, which seemed safe enough, because the administration and J. Edgar Hoover had always guarded them zealously from committee inspection. In this instance, however, Hoover did take the stand and testified that the file on Lattimore held nothing whatever to justify McCarthy's accusation. A procession of Communist and ex-Communist witnesses, Louis Budenz, Mrs. Bella Dodd, Earl Browder, and Mrs. Freda Utley, denied ever having heard of Lattimore as a Communist. To cap the climax, General MacArthur's chief of counterespionage testified about three investigations of Lattimore which had cleared him for full access to top secrets. The over-all result could hardly have been more conclusive.

Forced to give up on Lattimore, at least for the moment, McCarthy shifted to another professor, Philip C. Jessup, a member of the American delegation in the United Nations. He was, according to McCarthy, a notorious tool of the Communists. In proof, Jessup's connection with five, later six, Communist fronts was asserted. One was the Institute of Pacific Relations, where men of such respectability as President Ray Lyman Wilbur of Stanford, Juan Trippe of Pan American Airways, and Henry Luce of *Time, Life,* and *Fortune* were also to be found. The second had printed Jessup's name as a sponsor, but apparently without his consent, and in 1940 when no allegation had been made that the organization was un-American. As to the third, Jessup had merely lent his name, along with such reputables as H. V. Kaltenborn and George Fielding Eliot, in sponsorship of two dinners to which no valid objection could be made. The fourth organization, McCarthy had to admit, was not a Communist front. The fifth, Jessup could prove, was one to which he had never belonged. The sixth, the China Aid Society, he had not joined either, but his wife had, at the invitation of Madame Chiang Kai-shek.

Against these flimsy charges stood Jessup's record of truly distinguished service to the United States and the cause of freedom. As friend and biographer of Elihu Root and a one-time member of America First, Jessup actually could have claimed innocence by association. All this McCarthy disregarded, as he did Jessup's demonstrations that the specific charges were in error. The climax came in the fall of 1951 when Jessup's renomination as ambassador to the United Nations was before the Senate for approval. McCarthy went to the witness stand against it in the Senate subcommittee, staying there for ten hours with a rehearsal of all the charges and vilification he had been practicing over the past eighteen months. At the time it seemed that he overdid it and helped Jessup's chances with the committee. Harold Stassen seconded some of McCarthy's charges. On the other hand, Warren Austin, head of the American delegation to the United Nations, could not say enough in praise of Jessup, who was vouched for also in letters from Generals Clay, Marshall, and Eisenhower. When the committee came to a vote, however, it was 3 to 1 for McCarthy. All that President Truman could salvage was an interim appointment of Jessup after Congress adjourned.

The professor in government is a standard scapegoat, a fact which undoubtedly had bearing on McCarthy's picking on Lattimore and Jessup, though he must have been surprised at the vigor with which they fought back. In the summer of 1951, he trained his guns in an even more implausible direction, attacking the Secretary of Defense, General George C. Marshall, then perhaps the most respected figure in American government. As with many of McCarthy's accusations, it was difficult to determine just what the nub of the argument was, but it seemed to come down to putting the blame on Marshall for Russia's postwar gains in Asia and central Europe, for the failure to achieve a decisive military victory in Korea, and even for deliberately planning it that way. McCarthy spoke of "a conspiracy so immense and an infamy so black as to dwarf any such previous venture in the history of man." He linked Marshall and Acheson as partners in this "great conspiracy" directed from Moscow. Later, on television, he raised the question whether these conspirators were "stupid," "whether we've lost because of stumbling, fumbling idiocy, or because they planned it that way." The American people, he said, should decide "whether these individuals have been dupes or whether they are traitors." This was the tone of the attack.

One school of thought is that charges as false as these can do no harm, no matter how maliciously made—that only the truth can hurt. A variant on this theory is that a man of Marshall's character and stature cannot be hurt by the words of so despicable a person as a McCarthy. This particular performance, it is true, fell flat. Marshall did not dignify it with any reply. Commentators and editors, including some who were staunch Republicans, came out with blistering protests. Yet in the fetish of "impartial" news reporting—that is, of reporting what is said without any differentiation between truth and falsehood—this story made headlines all across the nation. Given that much encouragement, McCarthy felt free to repeat the accusation, quoting himself and embellishing on what he had said. Others picked up the refrain, the Chicago *Tribune*, for example. Marshall maintained his poise. In 1953 he was awarded the Nobel Peace Prize. Yet unnumbered Americans doubtless have a lingering doubt about him because of the calumny that McCarthy loosed.

The assault on Marshall illustrates McCarthy's recklessness. It does not put in view the range of his victims, the hyperactivity with which he jumped around the country spreading his charges, sometimes achieving his purpose through the darkness of innuendo, but often carrying his immunity with him through the device of quoting excerpts from his own speeches in the Senate, official committee reports, or testimony received. In such a campaign false charges were almost as good as true bills. Denials and rebuttals could not catch up with the charges and therefore could never cancel their effect. All the smoke that McCarthy was creating set up an impression that there must be some fire.

Also, either directly or indirectly his entire attack ricocheted to the Democratic administration. If there were Communists in government, the Democrats were to blame. If the State Department was playing into the hands of the Soviets, down with Truman and Acheson. If labor was infested, that too was the fault of the party in power. In all these years McCarthy was not able to expose a single Communist in government and to make that charge stick—he was not able to cash in on the reward of $25,000 that Senator Tydings offered him if he could do so. Politically, however, he became the darling of the outs. Wild though they were, his charges discomfited the Truman administration and especially the State Department. They made votes for the Republicans, and on that account even so upright a man as Senator Taft found it expedient to urge him to keep on, "and if one case didn't work, to bring up another."

To the impressive roster of persons stigmatized by him as Communists, McCarthy added another group—those who criticized him. They too, he asserted, were doing the work of Moscow. Into this category he found it possible to fit the Madison *Capitol Times* and the Milwaukee *Journal*, the Washington *Post*, and the St. Louis *Post-Dispatch*, Drew Pearson and the Alsop brothers, *Life* and *Time*, the Associated Press and the United Press, and, in due course, the *Saturday Evening Post* and the *Christian Science Monitor*. His pre-eminence in making the accusation of Communist was such that within a year or two the practice came to be known as McCarthyism.

An early proof of the utility of McCarthyism was the way in which McCarthy was able to turn it to his own protection. In his first years in the Senate, he had done several things that marred his popularity with his colleagues—for example, his bitter attack on Raymond Baldwin, the chairman of the Malmédy investigation. The new McCarthy of the anti-Communist phase constantly antagonized his fellow senators. His performance on the 205 or 57 or 81 or 8 or 1 Communist in the State Department baffled and disgusted many. In the summer of 1950 the Tydings committee made and documented the accusation that this whole charge of his was "a fraud and a hoax" and that he was guilty of "twisting, coloring, perverting, and distorting" the truth. McCarthy quickly took revenge. He plunged into the campaign in Maryland, where Tydings was up for re-election, and beat him badly. But the methods used—a tabloid full of misrepresentation, a shower of simulated personal postcards, a faked photograph of Tydings chatting with Earl Browder—antagonized more senators than they convinced. The illogic in McCarthy's attacks on Lattimore, Jessup, and especially Marshall, and the wildness of his charges so industriously spread across the land both irritated and offended.

It was left, however, for a freshman senator, William Benton of Connecticut, to try to beard the wild man from Wisconsin. On August 6, 1951, he introduced a ten-point bill of particulars culminating in a resolution to unseat McCarthy. The main charges were that he had committed perjury before the Tydings committee, had accepted $10,000 of "influence money" on the public housing issue, had tried "to hoax the Senate" with his accusation of Marshall, had tried to "frame" Tydings, had practiced "fraud and deceit" in the Maryland election, had not carried out promises to repeat without benefit of immunity libelous statements made on the floor of the Senate, had deliberately deceived in pretending to have an FBI document which J. Edgar Hoover later disavowed, had falsely accused Americans in the Malmédy atrocity, and had a perjurer still in his employ.

The Senate moved gingerly with this resolution, finally intrusting it to a committee, which McCarthy attempted to cajole and then to intimidate. Riled at his taunt that the committee was "dishonest" and that it might as well have "picked the pockets of the taxpayers," Senator Mike Monroney forced a showdown on the floor of the Senate. McCarthy countered with a resolution calling for an investigation of Benton. In the debate McCarthy set up another diversionary target by denouncing a respected member of the staff of the investigating committee, a tactic that incensed a number of senators on both sides of the aisle. By a vote of 60 to 0 the committee was instructed to proceed.

In the end, however, the inquiry was indecisive. A handful of Republican senators issued a Declaration of Conscience in protest at McCarthy's methods of irresponsible smearing and character assassination. Successive polls of political scientists and of newsmen ranked him ninety-sixth among the senators, that is, as the worst. To the mind untrained in the mysteries of the law, much of the evidence uncovered by the committee seemed damning, yet the Justice Department, after long delay, decided not to prosecute. McCarthy, it is true, got a lift from Senator McCarran's Internal Security Committee, which stepped in to pursue the Lattimore case and, with McCarthy's man Robert Morris as chief counsel, dug up some evidence more concrete than any that had come to light in 1950. This development may have deterred senators from moving vigorously against McCarthy. More broadly, however, there was good reason to fear his power and his retaliation.

The final dissolve was reminiscent of the one in Wisconsin six years earlier when the State Supreme Court ducked the question of the legality of McCarthy's candidacy. The Senate now chose to regard the 1952 elections as a referendum. The presidential canvass would be a barometer. How Benton fared in Connecticut would be a more direct sign, and, still more to the point, how McCarthy came out in Wisconsin.

The results, as is well known, fortified McCarthy right down the line. Eisenhower and the Republicans prevailed; Benton went down to defeat; and although the margin was narrow, the voters of Wisconsin sent McCarthy back to the Senate. It was plausible, furthermore, to interpret the election results as a mandate in favor of McCarthyism. Under the auspices of the Republican National Committee, the high priest of this cult had campaigned in a number of states in addition to Wisconsin. On top of that, the presidential candidates were clearly distinguishable on this issue. In his American Legion speech, for example, Stevenson was sharply critical. Eisenhower, in contrast, dramatically shared an Indiana platform with Jenner and tailored his Wisconsin speech to give no offense to McCarthy. McCarthyism may not have been the biggest issue in the campaign, but it certainly was one point.

With the organization of the new Congress in 1953 it became apparent that McCarthyism was going to be spread as well as strengthened. In the old days the Un-American Activities Committee of the House had achieved an approximate monopoly of probing for subversives and seeking headlines on the same. From 1950 through 1952, without benefit of a committee of his own, but with some public money as well as private for hiring investigators, McCarthy had usurped this role. Now the work became Hydra-headed. In the House, Harold Velde of Illinois was made chairman of the Un-American Activities Committee. He quickly gave indication that he would take the line of Dies, Rankin, and Thomas, together with a leaf or two from the junior senator from Wisconsin.

In the Senate the Internal Security Committee—which McCarran had dominated and used to grind a personal ax, as in the inquiry on Lattimore and American policy in Asia—now fell to Jenner of Indiana. He broadened its un-American scope considerably, aided by what appeared to be the administration's preference that this committee should be the chief searcher-out of subversives. At times the Jenner committee was given the palm for fairness and decorum. The basis, it should be remembered, was strictly relative. What the Jenner committee practiced may have been more refined, but it was McCarthyism nonetheless.

The Republicanizing of Congress had another consequence— the elevation of McCarthy to the chairmanship of the Committee on Government Operations. Now he could have more of an official staff for leg work, digging, and planning. Now he was officially licensed to pry into any facet of federal activity. Theoretically the justification was to check on the expenditure of the taxpayers' dollar and to see that it was not being wasted. It would be more consistent with McCarthyism to harp on Communism, to expose acts or operations that McCarthy could call favorable to Communism, to embarrass or hamstring agencies that he did not approve of, and, above all, to pillory individuals with the accusation that they were members or supporters of what he called "the Communist conspiracy" in the United States.

With the one-two-three punch of Velde, Jenner, and McCarthy, each at the helm of a congressional committee, McCarthyism was well set to flourish. As could have been predicted, they were not to be alone in its practice. Others pitched in, some of them in high office. The work of the three committees was too voluminous to follow in detail; representative examples will be noted.

The Velde committee, en banc, or by delegation, concerned itself with Hollywood, labor, the schools, and a variety of other matters. On the Hollywood front the first year's work was summarized in the harvest of persons denounced by witnesses as present or, most of them, former Communists. The Lucille Ball affair produced the bon mot from Congressman Jackson that in this case "the committee is departing from its usual procedure so that fact may be separated from rumor, and no damage done

Miss Ball." Unfortunately, it was not just a bon mot but an unintended confession as to the committee's customary methods.

Jackson and Velde brought the committee much notoriety
through remarks on extending the un-American probe to the
churches. Velde's offhand approval of such a move created a
furore. After Jackson lashed out at him for "serving God on
Sunday and Communism the rest of the week," Bishop Oxnam
demanded and got an audience with the committee. In a long
and stormy session he demolished the charges that the committee had on file against him. En route, however, he was trapped
into naming a couple of other clergymen as Communists or
possible Communists. The committee, furthermore, did not
give him a clean bill of health. By resolution it admitted that he
was not a Communist, but it did not absolve him of "serving
Communism." As Jackson put it, no case before the committee
is ever closed.

The histrionic peak for the Velde committee came after the
Brownell accusation that President Truman had knowingly kept
a Soviet spy in high office; in fact, had promoted him. Velde
hustled subpoenas to former President Truman, who answered
by radio and television; to Justice Tom Clark, who ignored the
summons; and to Governor James Byrnes, who stood haughtily
on states' rights.

The course of the Jenner committee was much more sedate,
but in some respects its impact was greater than that of Velde's
group. In higher education, for example, it brought in a procession of witnesses who refused to testify when questioned about
their past politics. The majority of these people were promptly
dismissed from their school and college posts. It also conducted
an inquiry into the alleged Communist backgrounds and connections of Americans on the staff of the United Nations. For
the Jenner committee the apogee came with the appearance of
Attorney-General Brownell to elaborate on the Harry Dexter
White charges he had thrown at former President Truman, and
of Brownell's subordinate, J. Edgar Hoover, as a corroborative

witness. The Jenner committee, it is true, was hardly more than the backdrop for these dramatics.

Month in and month out it was McCarthy who made the big headlines. He used what seemed an almost indiscriminate method, blazing away at one target, turning to another, moving on to some other victim, harking back to an earlier one, and often keeping two or three in the air at the same time. Volume rather than thoroughness was characteristic. He seldom if ever carried a line of questioning to a real conclusion. Instead, he relied on his staff investigators to marshal the selected details, and he used the actual hearings mostly to put hostile witnesses on the spot, to get them to claim the privilege of the Bill of Rights, whereupon he could brand them as "Fifth Amendment Communists," or to refuse in some other fashion and thus become subject to a citation for contempt.

A master at grabbing publicity, McCarthy worked all the angles. He gave advance releases on what was about to happen in committee hearings. He spread out the charges and disclosures so that they came in an endless flow. Exaggeration was his stock in trade, and with it he was an accessory both before and after the testimony. Perhaps as a legacy from his years on the bench, he was proficient in obiter dicta. His summaries, characterizations, and observations on testimony given, or on the degree of guilt to be read into the silence of particular witnesses, were works of art greatly embellishing what otherwise might have been a cold and drab record.

In midsummer the Democratic members of his subcommittee took violent exception to him on procedural grounds and refused to serve any longer on the investigating committee. They did not return until after the New Year. With or without these senators, McCarthy did much of the work alone, flanked only by his staff assistants. The impression was strong that he was the committee. He personalized the work in other ways, making a multitude of appearances at meetings, on the lecture platform, on radio and television, and always managing to bring in his pet subject. Though by no means his best performance, a highly remarkable one was his demanding and getting $300,000 worth of free time on all the stations that had carried President Truman's rejoinder to Brownell.

One issue much emphasized by McCarthy the committeeman was the trade which certain of our friends and allies were carrying on with Red China. It was limited to non-military goods, but McCarthy argued that any trade would tend to increase the military strength of the Chinese Reds. The English claimed, and our State Department agreed, that the trade benefited the Free World more than it did the Communists. Neither the United Nations nor any other international group had imposed a blockade of the China coast. McCarthy's position was that the United States should take this step on its own, and should enforce the blockade by boycotting any ships, ship companies, and shipowners that engaged in carrying cargoes to China, and by cutting off American aid to any nation participating in such trade.

The parade of staff and other witnesses yielded a certain amount of data on the Chinese import and export trade, the parties engaged, and the carriers. McCarthy interspersed moralizings on the infamy of this commerce. A considerable segment of American opinion—just what fraction is not recorded—agreed with him absolutely. Neither the White House nor the State Department was convinced, and when they did not jump to do his bidding by shutting down this trade, he excoriated the administration as well as those who were carrying on the actual traffic. The matter dragged on. McCarthy kept chanting a sort of refrain about how this shoring up of Red China ought to be stopped, but he got no action. Finally, on his nationwide hookup in supposed answer to Truman he interpolated a plea for telegrams to the White House protesting any more China trade. Strategically this turned out to be his worst mistake of 1953. A few thousand wires resulted, but the net consequence was merely to stiffen temporarily the Eisenhower-Dulles stand on the matter.

Through other hearings, probings, press releases, and public statements McCarthy sensationalized the issue of Communists in the Government Printing Office. Some evidence was produced, and more was hinted, that Printing Office employees had associated with Communists, had lived at the same address, and perhaps had been Communists. Certain witnesses declined to answer on the ground of the Fifth Amendment. The fanfare suggested that the Communists had a pipeline for delivery of the most secret of government documents hot from the linotype machines and the presses. No evidence of any such leakage was produced, and the management of the Printing Office stoutly denied that anything of the sort had occurred. No remedial legislation was proposed.

Rather similarly, McCarthy probed for possible Communists working as General Electric employees on government contracts. As a sort of aside, he blasted Harvard University for harboring an atomic physicist who admitted that he had belonged to a Communist group while at work on a secret atomic project but who refused to give the Jenner committee the names of the others in the group. Americans whose "children" were enrolled at Harvard should be informed of the incredible laxity in the administration of the university, McCarthy asserted. His leverage for threatening an exposé through the Committee on Operation of the Government was rather remote. It was that the taxpayers had a right to prescribe policy in an institution accorded tax exemption.

From his honeymoon McCarthy was dramatically recalled to launch an inquiry into an asserted Communist spy ring in the Army's scientific center at Fort Monmouth. Advance notices promised that espionage would be uncovered. The daily forecasts that McCarthy issued were in the same vein, though in his more sober moments he spoke more cautiously of "probing espionage." The evidence brought out fell far short of convincing the Army. After analyzing this evidence with the utmost care, Murrey Marder of the Washington *Post* gave it as his considered and documented judgment that the Fort Monmouth charges were a hoax, perpetrated by McCarthy and his aides, and perpetrated upon the American people.

The daily headlines, however, had spread the charges far and wide. In his annual report McCarthy boasted of his Fort Monmouth achievement and promised that in 1954 the work would go on and that the Communists "would bleed very freely." At year's end the box score was about as follows: No one had been indicted or convicted. No one had refused to testify. Although the charges had not been specified, some nineteen scientists had been suspended and another ten had been transferred to lesser assignments. Morale at the center was shaken. A number of needed scientists had quit their jobs and others would have done so except that they feared that a resignation would be interpreted as a confession of guilt. At Fort Monmouth McCarthy had demonstrated how a congressional investigator running amuck can demobilize a government operation.

In February, 1954, he opened a second front against the Army. He demanded to know who had promoted and then honorably discharged a dentist, Irving Peress, on the eve of his being haled before the McCarthy subcommittee for questioning on his political ties. As it developed, Peress invoked the Fifth Amendment, whereupon McCarthy, with what might have been regret, observed that in Russia an officer who declined to answer would be executed at once. McCarthy did get Brigadier General Ralph Zwicker on the stand and reviled him for shielding Peress and the officers who had promoted and released him. Secretary of the Army Stevens thereupon took over, denounced the morale-shattering techniques that McCarthy was using, and issued a general order to officers to disregard subpoenas from McCarthy's committee. This beginning, however, was far braver than the ending. Cornered by Republican stalwarts, Stevens was persuaded to back down. The President, when he returned from a California vacation, voiced confidence in the officers of the Army, but let McCarthy have his way. Cartoonist Herblock, with good grasp on the realities, showed Stevens surrendering his sword to McCarthy and Eisenhower challenging the Senator by drawing a white feather from the scabbard.

Stevens' initial determination to fight for the integrity of the

Army may well have been inspired by the spectacle of what had happened in the Department of State. McCarthy's attempt to dictate an international ban on all trade with Red China, it is true, had not succeeded, though politically even it may have yielded him certain dividends. In other sorties against State he had had better success. Although High Commissioner James B. Conant and his predecessor John J. McCloy had volunteered the best of character indorsement, McCarthy brought about the ouster of Theodore Kaghan, a most effective worker in the American interest in Germany. McCarthy also moved in on the department's Information Service libraries.

The preliminary move was a whirlwind tour of the establishments in Europe by McCarthy's young henchmen, Roy Cohn and David Schine. Their mad dash to and through the Continent had its comic aspects; the English press could not resist the routine "Positively, Mr. Cohn? Absolutely, Mr. Schine." The hilarious, however, was overshadowed by the sinister. At Bonn, for example, these emissaries pilloried Kaghan. Among the souvenirs of their trip they also brought back a list of "Communist books" in the overseas libraries.

McCarthy now took over, blasting the State Department for permitting such infiltration of these libraries whose purpose was to win friends and influence peoples toward the American plans and program. He demanded an accounting. He wanted to know who had made such a decision. Why had the taxpayers' money been diverted to such an end? Was it not obvious that part of the royalties paid to Communist authors would find its way to the coffers of the Communist conspiracy?

A list of some 140 titles was at length released. The objection, it turned out, was not on the basis of content, but merely because the author or editor or illustrator was assertedly a Communist or a member of one or more asserted Communist fronts. The head of the Information Service and the higher officials of the State Department wavered before the attack. They protested, but they issued a bewildering series of orders and counterorders. They did withdraw the criticized books. Eleven books were actually and literally burned. On the stand Conant was resolute to the extent of drawing a slur from McCarthy that he was obviously not competent to hold the job to which he had been appointed; yet Conant was not nearly so explicit in support of intellectual freedom as he often had been while president of Harvard.

In a speech at Dartmouth College, President Eisenhower spoke out forthrightly against the bookburners. Choosing to be strictly literal about it, and to disregard the more important symbolic meaning of the word "bookburning," McCarthy answered, "Who, me? I haven't burned a single book." The American Library Association countered with a ringing declaration on freedom to read. Some adjustments were made. For example, the President decreed that Dashiell Hammett's mystery stories were fit for inclusion in the libraries. But if there was a general restoration of the books that had been withdrawn, it was not publicized. A justifiable impression was created that the information centers had been reduced to propaganda agencies vending a bill of goods rather than a cross-section of the truth about America. Even more alarming was the disparity between the words at Dartmouth and the decisions at Washington. The voice, one would think, must have been almost completely jammed by the executive actions.

A postscript in February, 1954, concerns the removal of still another title, the *Collected Works of Thomas Jefferson*. Including as they do the Declaration of Independence and the Virginia Statute of Religious Freedom, Jefferson's writings are in their own right a worthy target of McCarthyism. Removal, however, was on the subordinate ground that the editor was suspect.

In the fall of 1952 the Republican high command embraced McCarthyism as a major element in the presidential campaign. Eisenhower displayed a warm togetherness with Jenner and McCarthy. A fortnight before election day Nixon made a special point of impugning Stevenson's patriotism or judgment because in the spring of 1949 he had told the truth about Hiss's reputation. Finally, for a climax speaker on a nationwide hookup the Republicans chose McCarthy.

Notwithstanding these signs, there were some who questioned that the Eisenhower administration would countenance Mc-Carthyism. At the outset there was room for doubt, or, if one judged merely by the President's words, there was assurance that it would not be practiced or permitted. Yet coming in as it did with new broom rampant, intent on cleaning up "the mess" in Washington, the new administration was under temptation to look for Communists in every bureau. The exaggerated talk about "the mess" was a leaf out of McCarthyism. To cry Communist and soft on Communist was an easy recourse. On a point or two, notably the trade-with-Red-China issue, Eisenhower stood firm. On a larger number of points it appeared that the administration could live at peace with McCarthyism. In at least two major episodes the administration went further and practiced McCarthyism on a scale that McCarthy himself had not achieved.

Brownell's attack on President Truman, in a speech that had been cleared with the White House, was one such instance. It was made first as an unparticularized charge, but putting Truman in the worst possible light. Within hours the White House had mimeographed supplements ready for the press. When taxed for accusing Truman of treasonable conduct, Brownell substituted a charge of blindness almost to the point of willful blindness. Appearing before the Jenner committee and the television cameras to substantiate what he had said, Brownell presented his own résumé of a still-shrouded FBI report, together with supporting comment from J. Edgar Hoover. That there was evidence in 1946 on which Harry Dexter White could have been convicted of espionage was far from demonstrated. That it had been made known to Truman that he was a spy was even further from being demonstrated. With only such evidence brought out as Brownell chose to declassify, the victim, President Truman, was given an unplayable lie. In his broadcast on November 16 he made a valiant effort to blast out. In this his success was far from complete, but the logic of his analysis of what had just been done to him was convincing. He said:

It is now evident that the present administration has fully embraced, for political advantage, McCarthyism. I am not referring to the senator from Wisconsin—he is only important in that his name has taken on a dictionary meaning in the world. It is the corruption of truth, the abandonment of our historic devotion to fair play. It is the abandonment of the "due process" of law. It is the use of the big lie and the unfounded accusation against any citizen in the name of Americanism and security. It is the rise to power of the demagogue who lives on untruth; it is the spread of fear and the destruction of faith in every level of our society.

This is not a partisan matter. This horrible cancer is eating at the vitals of America and it can destroy the great edifice of freedom.

A second flagrant example of McCarthyism practiced by the Eisenhower administration was in the misleading claims on the number of subversives ousted from federal jobs. An executive order in April, 1953, modified the loyalty program that President Truman had set up. It extended the coverage to all departments and did away with the general appeals board. The other principal change was to lump together the various grounds for dismissal under the general heading of security risks. Suspicion of disloyalty was now grouped with suspicion of unreliability on various lesser grounds such as intemperance. The system might protect a suspect from being clouded as disloyal, and the press at the time welcomed it as a kindly gesture. It should have been elementary that a definition that is loose can be pulled with equal ease in either direction. Leading Republicans proceeded to stretch it the other way.

On October 23 the White House press secretary released a statement that under the security program 1,456 federal employees had been separated. He did not remind that "security" as here used covered a multitude of faults less heinous than disloyalty. Party spokesmen quickly picked up the refrain. The Postmaster-General and the President's chief legal counsel, for example, boasted about these dismissals with the clear inference that all were subversives. On December 16, Governor

Thomas E. Dewey extolled the progress toward a government "not infested with spies and traitors." "In less than eleven months," he went on to say, "the Department of Justice had discovered and dismissed 1,456 security risks planted in the government of the United States under Democratic administrations." McCarthy assured a television audience that "practically all" of the 1,456 "were removed because of Communist connections and activities or perversion," and on a later broadcast he set the figure at more than 90 per cent.

Meanwhile, all attempts to get an authoritative breakdown failed. The President side-stepped the question or referred reporters to the Attorney-General, who, on his part, would not meet the press. The chairman of the Civil Service Commission, Philip Young, who had more direct jurisdiction in the matter, brushed such questions aside with the assertion that he could not see why anyone would be interested "whether a person was discharged for being disloyal or for being a drunk."

By going to the various departments a Washington reporter found that many resignations and even a few terminations by death were included in the tally of so-called dismissals. It also came to light that some of the departmental figures did not agree with those reported. The Navy, for example, counted eight civilian workers dismissed and twelve suspended as security risks, whereas the Civil Service Commission had listed 192. Under pressure the Navy accepted the figure, though watering it down as applying to former employees "against whom a security question existed." Other departments were even more critical of the commission's figures.

In his State of the Union message on January 7, 1954, however, the President spoke with pride of "dismissals under the security program" which by that date, he said, had mounted to 2,200. His words set off a new flurry of embellishments by party orators. A week later the President admitted that the figure included employees who had resigned without knowing that it had ever been intimated that they were a risk to security. Representative Katherine St. George, a Republican from New York, meanwhile reported that she had it from high authority that not more than 10 per cent of those counted were under suspicion as subversive. Testimony from various departments at hearings on appropriations raised further doubts.

Therefore, on March 2, Chairman Young submitted an official score card which claimed disposal of 2,427 security risks, of whom 1,074 had been dismissed and 1,353 resigned, and of whom 194 were classified as sex perverts, while for 383 there was information in the files "indicating, in various degrees, subversive activities, subversive associations, or membership in subversive organizations." Even as applied to these 383, Young's label of "subversive" seems ever so much wider than any justifiable meaning of the term. This goes far toward explaining how his agency and department subtotals could be so far in excess of what these same departments were reporting in direct testimony to congressional committees. Whatever haul of disloyal employees there was, it clearly was far below Young's figure, and the number of Communists caught, if any, was small indeed.

Even though it had been decided not to brand dismissees as loyalty risks, the administration might have been justified in reporting the number of such persons removed. No such justification existed for padding the totals by including employees separated on other grounds, or for seizing on any of these numbers as suggestive of the administration's bag of actual or would-be spies or traitors. Significantly, not one of these ousted employees was indicted or prosecuted, not even for perjury.

The Lincoln Day dinners of 1954 were marked by another burst of McCarthyism. As chief speaker at nine of these dinners McCarthy himself set the plane. His topic was "Twenty Years of Treason" and his theme, as he phrased it, was: "The hard fact is that those who wear the label Democrat wear it with the stain of an historic betrayal," for it is "a political label stitched with the idiocy of a Truman, rotted by the deceit of an Acheson, corrupted by the red slime of a White." Other party spokesmen took up the chant; indeed, Dewey had taken almost this same pitch in his speech at Hartford a couple of months earlier. The

President sanctimoniously washed his hands of this lumping of all Democrats as traitors; yet to every indication this was the campaign line predetermined by the party managers over whom he was the titular head.

These episodes, disturbing as they are, by no means bring out the full sway of McCarthyism. Its menace was not just in the increasing skill, effrontery, and abandon with which the eponymous senator practiced it, and not just in the avidity with which other politicians and, indeed, a party jumped upon this bandwagon. The more arresting fact was and is that the American people, or at least a substantial number of them, seemed to be taken in by McCarthyism or intimidated by it. In the public mind the domestic threat of Communism inflated to match our whole fear of Communist Russia. A thing so traditional as criticism of the majority view came to be confused with disloyalty. Mere accusation came to be accepted as proof, and guilt to be assessed without trial or evidence. Even among those who remembered our birthright of freedom, distressingly many were silent.

The lodgment of these errors and this cravenness in the hearts of the people may be regarded as at once the cause of the American descent to McCarthyism and its most disheartening aspect.

To be sure, a wishful review of the Senator's hectic career identifies many points at which he and perhaps his ism so easily could have been halted. If the Wisconsin Supreme Court had only enforced the law against judges running for office; if the Wisconsin Democrats had not helped take the Republican nomination away from La Follette; if the Senate had acted on the true bill returned by the Tydings committee; if it had faced up to the Benton charges instead of referring them to the Connecticut and Wisconsin voters; if the liberal Republicans who prevailed in the Chicago convention had not gone over to an alliance with McCarthy; if the Senate had called him to heel early in 1953; if the Attorney-General had gone to court with the tax evasion charges; if the Eisenhower administration had demoted him from his position as party keynoter; if the President, instead of "never dealing with personalities" had been willing to have a quick showdown on bookburning or Fort Monmouth or General Zwicker or the "twenty years of treason" —if any of these opportunities had been seized, McCarthy might not have risen so high.

This train of thought, in effect, sets up a series of scapegoats in Wisconsin and Washington to whom we can transfer the full onus for the inflation of McCarthy. The escape, however, is not that easy. In almost every instance the decision not to move in on him was a political one. It recognized the forces behind him— incidentally, the Texas millionaires and the reactionary press, but far more important, the formidable array of public sentiment. In last analysis, therefore, the failure for so long to bring him under proper restraint was because not enough people had enough of the will to do it. The blame for McCarthyism, as Edward R. Murrow so effectively pointed out, rests with every one of us who did not straighten up and act like a free man.

6. Toward a Police State

Alongside the American revulsion against Communists runs another feeling almost as widely held, that something has been wrong with our handling of American Communists. It is not a question of whether we have been too soft or too tough. More basically it is that the measures taken have been awkward and inefficient. They have been prostituted to serve other purposes, have gravely damaged innocent persons, and have cast aside cardinal principles. Ostensibly aimed at one small element in the population, they have wrought a much broader devastation and have weakened the whole fabric of our society.

These unfortunate consequences can be traced in part to steps taken within the framework of government. In our day the automatic response to almost any problem is to say, There ought to be a law. In that mood we have searched the inherited stockpile of old laws for regulations that could be applied to Communists and suspected Communists. Several workable restraints have been found—the perjury laws, for example, and the disqualification of parties from a place on the ballot when their vote falls below a certain minimum.

Along with these controls many new laws have been proposed. Bills and ordinances by the hundreds have gone into the legislative hoppers, and at the national, state, and local levels a considerable number have been made law. On the whole these enactments have been more vitriolic than ingenious. They have the character of acts of passion rather than of calm deliberation. Each session of Congress sees Communist-control measures introduced, and the lengths to which this kind of law-making will go cannot be foretold.

The high tide in such legislating came in the pandemonium of the closing days of the Eighty-third Congress, in August, 1954, after the Senate had exhausted itself on the question of the give-away of atomic energy patent rights to private industry. Then it was that Congress voted the death penalty for peacetime espionage. It also qualified the Fifth Amendment by authorizing the courts (though not the Attorney-General alone) to use the immunity device to force witnesses to testify. It set up Communist infiltration as a further ground for restrictions on labor unions. Through the Humphrey Amendment, rhetorically and purportedly, though not quite in actuality, it outlawed the Communist party.

This amendment, which as introduced went the whole distance of making Communist membership a felony, undoubtedly stemmed from Democratic smarting under the taunt of "twenty years of treason." A major purpose was to block that metaphor in the coming campaign, in which, incidentally, Humphrey was to be up for re-election. Alert to its political potential, half the Democratic senators and the one Independent stampeded to get on the list of sponsors of the amendment.

Some senators rose to speak against it. They pointed out that it would make existing subversive-control measures unworkable, that it was probably unconstitutional, that it made involuntary action or even inaction a crime, and that under its operation American freedom and security would be decreased rather than increased. Yet such is the magic of the anti-Communist shibboleth that only Senator Kefauver dared vote against it.

The House version differed, and in conference the provision making mere membership a felony was deleted. As adopted, the measure was a concoction of floor-written rewordings and revisions, and the lawmakers did not have a correct text before them until many days after they had voted. The Justice Department evinced no enthusiasm but withheld comment until the law as enacted could be studied in detail. President Eisenhower is said to have characterized the measure as "a can of worms"—and this from a dry-fly fisherman. But he signed it into law, and in his televised résumé of the work of the Eighty-third Congress he lumped it in with the enactments that swelled his so-called batting average.

Even without this 1954 packet of bills enacted, there had been entered in the statutes a formidable quantity of sumptuary law, law for the regulation of political and moral conduct. To date, even with the Humphrey Amendment, we have not in so many words made simple membership in the Communist party a crime. We have preferred to go at it piecemeal, with the same quality of mercy that is present in cutting the dog's tail off an inch at a time. Yet our course has been relentless. Our clear and avowed purpose has been to put the party and its partisans out of business, and we have come closer to outright proscription than ever before for any minority or faction.

Furthermore, as their contribution to the drive to save America from the American Communists, government officials both high and low have stretched their discretionary power about as far as it will go. Sumptuary administrative and judicial action has joined hands with sumptuary legislation. In both, the campaign has frequently involved devices that borrow from and border on the methods of the police state. Without wanting to become a police state, we have let the pursuit of Communists carry us a good distance down the road that leads to exactly that destination.

Many Americans, although recognizing that extreme and unusual powers of government were being applied, have been inclined to take comfort in the thought that, after all, it was happening just to Communists, for whom the worst would be none too good. In point of fact, however, the policing has not been anywhere nearly that discriminate. Some of the measures even appear to have hurt actual Communists not at all and to have forced persons strongly opposed to Communism to bear the brunt.

Even if the enforcement of these measures in every instance had gone true to the announced mark, there would still be good reason for patriotic citizens to be much disturbed. The best possible assurance, indeed the only reliable assurance, that a government will adhere to fair practice is the actual record of its behavior. If it departs from that standard in one case or for one set of individuals, there is no certainty that it will not do so in other cases and against other groups. A citizen alert to the dangers of the police state may well remember Jesus' words, "Inasmuch as ye have done it unto one of the least of these my brethren, ye have done it unto me." Brought down to the arena of government, this truth is that each citizen is vitally involved when any other citizen is misused.

In the government-operated program to rid the nation of Communists, the numerical favorite has been the test oath. This facet of the program illustrates society's habit of shunning invention and instead, wherever possible, reviving some ancient device. When Protestantism burst upon Europe in the days of Luther, Calvin, and Loyola, it set up bitter controversies over political as well as doctrinal heresy. As the contest went on, kings and courts bent on stamping out nonconformity turned to the device of the test oath, a required denial of unorthodox religious belief, but in effect also a required political denial. An earlier instance, likewise political as well as religious, was the Roman demand that suspects deny Christ.

The framers of our government well knew the noxious effects of the test oath as it had been used in England. They wanted no such thing in the United States, and to make sure they specified that "no religious test shall ever be required as a qualification to any office or public trust under the United States."

The modern revival of the required disclaimer oath came, appropriately enough, in Nazi Germany and Fascist Italy. Hitler,

Goebbels, and Mussolini were astute enough to realize that mere foreswearing of anti-Nazi or anti-Fascist belief would not make stauncher Nazis and Fascists. They used the device primarily to degrade and discredit potential opponents, and with much success.

The loyalty question, it is true, had been raised in the United States just after the close of the First World War. The agitation was chiefly against Socialists, as witness the expulsion of five elected Socialists from the New York Assembly and refusal of Congress to seat Victor Berger, duly elected from Wisconsin. Measures such as the Lusk Act in New York opened avenues for frightening and pressuring teachers into strict conformity. The idea of an anti-Socialist oath, however, seems not to have occurred to anyone.

In the thirties, with totalitarianism on the increase in Europe, the American loyalty drive entered a new phase in which the chief aim appears to have been to try to block the program of the New Deal. An element in the campaign was to insist on the salute to the flag as a daily ritual in every school and on teachers being put on oath to support the Constitution. Some fourteen states did enact requirement of a positive pledge of allegiance from public school teachers, usually in the wording of the oath of office taken by public servants from the earliest days of the republic. Like the salute to the flag, such an oath or affirmation can be inspiring. It is an earnest of good intention and was so regarded by most of the teachers who were asked to take it.

Without benefit of an oath of any other type we went through the Second World War, triumphantly and without so much as an incident of sabotage. Suddenly, in the postwar era, the test oath, the disclaimer oath, the oath of denial, became epidemic.

This new oath is in the tradition of the Roman grilling of the Christians, the early English testing against dissenters, and the Nazi insistence on conformity. It derives also from what the legislative investigators liked to call their $64 question.

Today's test oath takes a thousand forms. It ranges from five words to a page or more of fine print. Its essence, however, is

the negative statement, "I am not. . . ." Sometimes this is extended into the past, "I am not . . . and I have never been . . ."
or "I am not . . . and within the past five years I have not been.
. . ."

The specification of what must be denied varies widely from
oath to oath. In most instances the emphasis is on denial of
membership in the Communist party, but at times it is more
vaguely of being a Communist, a member of any Communist-
front organization, of any totalitarian organization, of any organization cited as subversive, or of any organization committed
to the overthrow of the government by force and violence. The
demand sometimes is for denial of belief or advocacy of overthrow of the government by force and violence, or of being under commitments that would render one less than a free agent,
or of knowingly being a member of an organization of which
any of the above could be asserted. Not uncommonly the oath
tries to incorporate all these denials.

With practice the lawmakers have been able to make these
oaths more and more labyrinthine. They cast them in the complicated jargon of legalism, remove any of the inspirational quality contained in the traditional pledge of allegiance, and instead
make them instruments of entrapment from which perjury actions might possibly stem.

Certain states—Oregon, for example—have seen no useful
purpose in collecting sworn statements from people who are not
and have never been accused of being Communists. Elsewhere,
the requirement of such oaths has luxuriated.

Next door, in California, there was a beginning in 1947 when
Los Angeles County called on every employee to take a test oath
disclaiming Communist party membership and to check off on
a supplied list his memberships in suspected organizations. The
city of Los Angeles, the state university, and various other state
and local units followed suit. In 1950 the legislature enacted
such a requirement for all who were to be paid for any services
by the state. Because the state constitution explicitly forbade any
oath but the time-honored positive pledge from the governor,

the legislators, and the judges, they were exempted from the new oath of denial. It, however, was to be exacted from everyone else, down to the most casual state employee—for example, an infant who worked as a model for an art class. In 1952 this same test oath was written into the state constitution. In 1953 additional legislation required like oaths or affidavits from veterans, charitable bodies, and churches as the price for the customary tax exemptions. Through malice or inadvertence the oath was also inserted in the form for declaring property holdings to the county assessors, and many citizens not legally required to swear this particular oath were maneuvered into doing so. A conservative estimate is that half the voters in California have signed one or more of these oaths. Notwithstanding all this swearing, no one has been convicted or indicted or publicly accused of having perjured himself in this oath-taking.

The oath of denial, miscalled a loyalty oath, has spread most of the way across the land. It has cropped up in towns and villages, in local school districts, in state colleges and universities, as a condition for state employment, and at several levels of federal operation, for example, as applied to labor union officers under the Taft-Hartley Act. These oath requirements have been criticized as bills of attainder, denials of due process, invasions of the right of silence that is a corollary of the right of free speech, and in other respects unconstitutional. Several have been thrown out by the courts. In other instances, the courts have ruled them within the law. The deeper question concerns the wisdom of all this insistence on sworn denials. There is little evidence of Communists caught or demobilized but much evidence of non-Communists harassed and penalized, of lowered morale on the part of many public servants, and of depreciation of the traditional freedoms.

Historic examples are often cited of how behavior has been controlled by the swearing of a great oath. It happened to King David with his oath to Bathsheba, to Richard the Lion-Hearted, and to the Stanford Vow Boys, who confounded the experts by going on to an undefeated season on the gridiron. These historic oaths, however, were all prospective. They looked to the future. They pledged determination, effort, and fortitude thenceforth. Today's test oath is not on this order. It looks back. Its promises relate only to the past. Its useful effect is no more than if we were to collect an oath from a governor at the end of his term, or if a team at the end of the season were to clasp hands and covenant that they had never deviated from the will to win.

Another example of search for security through legislation is in the immigration and alien controls of the McCarran and McCarran-Walter Acts of 1950 and 1952. They accept the doctrine that only such immigrants should be admitted as are apt to be readily assimilated. Toward that end they re-enact, with some modifications, the national-origins quota system of 1924. More distinctive is the great stress put upon political desirability. They go much further than any earlier American laws to erect barriers against the entrance of thoughts and beliefs. They set up an Ellis Island for ideas.

Interception of persons whose alleged taint is in their ideas is bound to be difficult. Significantly, the methods set up by the McCarran Acts strikingly resemble those of the congressional investigating committees. Past association is accepted as compelling evidence. Anonymous accusation is received and used. Doubts are resolved against the applicant, which means there is presumption of guilt. There is provision for appeal and review, but here also the weighting is against the applicant. Other parts of the code authorize like methods in denaturalization and deportation procedures.

The McCarran Acts snarled the entrance rules so that international scientific gatherings in the United States became nearly impossible, reduced immigration to a trickle, and virtually closed the United States as a haven for political refugees. These laws bar good prospects for useful citizenship—war brides, for example—who in their youth had been involuntarily enrolled in totalitarian organizations. They have resulted in imprisonment or exile of aliens with a record of as much as thirty or forty years of residence or even of supposed citizenship in the United States.

These laws may have excluded some individuals who would have voted Communist. Any service they may have rendered toward preventing totalitarians from taking over the United States is more than counterbalanced by the fears they have aggravated within our nation and the offense they have given to our friends and allies. In his veto message, President Truman forecast these baleful effects, and President Eisenhower, as early as February, 1953, reminded that "we are—one and all—immigrants, or the sons and daughters of immigrants." He called on Congress to revise the statute so as to make it "faithful to our basic ideas of freedom and fairness to all." His plea fell on deaf ears. After the suppression of the Hungarian rebellion in 1956, an emergency measure opened the door for some fifty thousand refugees, but Congressman Walter warned that for all anyone knew they might all be Communists.

Another even more drastic measure that could be invoked against the American Communists had been enacted in 1940, prior to American involvement in the Second World War but at a time when the problem of national security was in the forefront of public attention. This law, the Smith Act, was reminiscent of the rash of criminal syndicalism laws of 1917–20 with which several states attempted to combat the Industrial Workers of the World. In essence these laws asserted that where two or three were gathered together for the purposes of the IWW they were guilty of conspiracy to overthrow the government by force. The result was a long list of convictions, not for doing the deed, but for conspiring to do it. The Smith Act carried this doctrine two steps further, making it a crime to advocate forcible overthrow of the government or to organize or belong to an organization which so advocates.

This section of the Smith Act was first applied, ironically enough, to curb the more moderate Trotskyite faction of American Communists. At Minneapolis in 1941 some twenty-nine members of the Socialist Workers party were brought to trial and convicted. They asked for review by the Supreme Court but did not get it, and as the Second World War was drawing toward a close they served out their sentences.

It was not until 1949, in the burgeoning anti-Communism of the Cold War, that the Smith Act was applied to the central phalanx of American Communists. Then, in what is known as the Dennis case, eleven principal figures in the party were brought to trial in New York. The trial stretched out over nine months. Identification of the eleven as top functionaries in the party was relatively easy. On this the government was conclusive. The prosecution did not allege any overt act, but its main effort went to the point that the Communist party did in fact purpose violent overthrow of the government, which the accused vigorously denied. The point of law with which the court really wrestled was whether presence and association two stages removed from any possibility of an overt act could properly be called a crime.

Judge Harold R. Medina instructed the jury that the defendants could be held guilty provided it was established that they intended, not necessarily immediately, to seek to overthrow the government by force. The jury so found, and the Circuit Court, with Judge Learned Hand writing the opinion, upheld the convictions. His reasoning accepted the doctrine of "clear and present danger" which Justice Holmes had advanced, and extended it into the realm of probability. If conspiracy creates a sufficiently grave and probable danger, Hand was ready to call it treason.

On review, the Supreme Court in a 6 to 2 division found the law constitutional. It took three separate opinions to explain the reasoning of the majority. It came down, however, to approximately this: the threat posed by Communism was held to be so great, the crisis so perilous, that the constitutional guaranty of the First Amendment must give way. Justice Frankfurter, at least by implication, was ready to have the act enforced because in the opinion of Congress the need to guard against advocacy of revolution was greater than the need to preserve freedom to speak and teach. Justice Jackson, though doubtful of the worth of the particular measure, held that it was unreasonable for the court to attempt to prophesy that a world-wide revolutionary conspiracy was sure to fail. Chief Justice Vinson and his co-signers backed off from the position that probability of success was the issue. Therein they took leave of Holmes and Brandeis, of Hand, and of Frankfurter and Jackson. To them it sufficed that there had been a finding of probability of an attempt to overthrow the government, and that the defendants had organized to advocate, and with intent, that such an attempt should be made. For these justices a "clouded and remote" danger was as good as a "clear and present" danger.

In dissent, Justice Black protested that laws suppressing freedom of speech and press could not be sustained merely on the basis of "reasonableness," thereby diluting the First Amendment to a mere admonition. In quick analysis of the case he pointed out that the petitioners "were not charged with an attempt to overthrow the Government. They were not charged with overt acts of any kind designed to overthrow the Government. They were not even charged with saying anything or writing anything designed to overthrow the Government. The charge was that they agreed to assemble and to talk and publish certain ideas at a later date: The indictment is that they conspired to organize the Communist Party and to use speech or newspapers and other publications in the future to teach and advocate the forcible overthrow of the Government. No matter how it is worded," Justice Black continued, "this is a virulent form of prior censorship of speech and press, which I believe the First Amendment forbids. I would hold §3 of the Smith Act authorizing this prior restraint unconstitutional on its face and as applied." Justice Douglas was equally emphatic: "Free speech—the glory of our system of government—should not be sacrificed on anything less than plain and objective proof of danger that the evil advocated is imminent."

In some quarters the decision was hailed as the death knell of the Communist party. Its immediate result was to open a way to fine and imprison the party leaders, and within a few months several score were indicted and convicted. In 1957, however, the Supreme Court freed several persons thus convicted in California and thereby reversed part at least of the precedent set in the Dennis case. In other quarters the decision in the Dennis case had been viewed as the death knell of the First Amendment because it rationalized a method of setting aside the constitutional guaranties of freedom of speech and assembly.

In several instances the courts have called a halt on excesses committed in the name of loyalty and security. Because of such rulings even before 1957 the courts loomed up as the chief bulwark of the freedoms in this time of stress. Quite understandably, however, the sentiments that pervade the nation to some extent penetrate the courtroom. In common with most citizens, judges are aware of international Communism and consider that much of its menace is personified by the American party members. On the bench, therefore, there has been a willingness to explore for interpretations that would permit rigorous and even discriminatory restraints. Many such have been found, ranging from expanding the Holmes aphorism on "clear and present danger" to getting around the ban against forcing a wife to testify against her husband. Praise of the courts as uncompromising defenders of the freedoms has to be tempered because of this approval of short cuts through the older forms of due process.

The states and their subdivisions, as indicated above, have kept pace with the federal government in drafting and requiring test oaths. As to immigration they have no authority and therefore have not enacted a series of little McCarran laws. The safeguarding of national security as undertaken in the Smith Act likewise seems logically to belong to the federal government. Nevertheless, under the police power, or perhaps on the theory that treason and conspiracy to commit treason are where you find them, the states have moved extensively into the field of legislation purportedly designed to insure internal security. In the Nelson case, the Pennsylvania Supreme Court ruled that this field belongs to the federal government.

State and local laws, ordinances, and regulations with this announced aim still are myriad. Many of them use the device of a test oath. Many also employ the test of association. Another common characteristic is an animus against unorthodoxy, dissent, and nonconformity. Examples are the determination to eliminate any study of the United Nations or UNESCO from the schools, to suppress left-wing publications, and to discourage open discussion involving any challenge of the status quo.

These state and local laws have taken certain books off the shelves. They have prevented the holding of certain meetings. They have stricken elements from the study program in particular schools. They have evicted certain individuals from public or semipublic housing. They have withdrawn long-existing tax exemptions from certain individuals and organizations. They have subjected others to long and expensive litigation and have deprived still others of their jobs. Upon a good many persons the impact of these laws has been heavyhanded. Literally millions of persons have been jostled toward stricter conformity, and thousands have had their earning power cut down or demolished. The hardships inflicted have been severe; yet in all the forty-eight states there is hardly a person who has been brought to trial for violation of any of these myriad local statutes and then tried and convicted and sentenced to fine or imprisonment. If protection against violent overthrow of the government is really the aim, the punishment should be direct and official. The persons who by implication of these laws are a threat to the nation's security should not be at large. If, however, the real purpose of these laws is to narrow the exercise of free speech, free press, freedom of religion, and freedom to assemble, they do make sense, for that is their effect.

Examples could be endlessly multiplied. From its earliest existence as a state, California followed the practice of exempting churches from taxation on properties used for religious purposes. In 1953, as one among several "security" enactments, the legislature made this exemption contingent upon the filing of a test oath, a disclaimer of disloyalty on behalf of the particular church. To the non-legalistic mind this requirement seems a clear violation of the principle of separation of church and state, but in 1957 the California Supreme Court upheld it. The United States Supreme Court may ultimately find it unconstitutional, but meanwhile it operates as a pressure for political orthodoxy in the churches.

New York's Feinberg Act has had far more publicity. Hastily enacted in 1949, it instructed the state Board of Regents to make a list of organizations which teach or advocate violent overthrow of the government. Membership in any such organization then would constitute prima facie evidence for dismissal from any position in the New York schools. By a margin of 6 to 3 the Supreme Court in 1951 upheld the statute. The majority reasoned that the schools are a sensitive area, that the inquiry into associations was reasonable, and that although teachers have the right "to assemble, speak, think, and believe as they will," they do not have the right to work in the school system on their own terms. "If they do not choose to work on such terms," the court ruled, "they are at liberty to retain their beliefs and associations and go elsewhere."

The New York *Times* had protested the "blunderbuss" character of the measure and objected to its use of the "untenable and illiberal theory" of guilt by association. When the Adler case reached the Supreme Court, Justice Frankfurter dissented on jurisdictional grounds, and Justices Black and Douglas excoriated the law as based "on a principle repugnant to our society." They recognized that the prior condemnation of an organization made the hearing granted the individual member or associate almost pointless. And they foresaw a serious loss to society through the blighting of academic freedom. By a margin of 6 to 3, however, the court upheld the statute.

Alongside the new laws for policing political behavior there have been executive orders and administrative procedures that proved even more officious. One such is on display in the workings of the Immigration Service. The enacted laws are partly responsible, especially as they assign the duty of intercepting what McCarthy liked to call "Communist thinkers." But here the statutes are abetted by the procedures that have been developed. An example is in the formidable questionnaires and checking preliminary to issuance of a visa. Protecting its informers, the Immigration Service often does not make known what charges it has received. In 1951–52, without hearings, it refused admission to some two thousand applicants.

Deportation of aliens operates on a similar basis, with doubts resolved against rather than for the individual. Appeals are heard before the self-same agency which made the original ruling, and in other respects the safeguards against arbitrariness are clearly inadequate. The Department of Justice has also found ways of applying the same kind of sanctions against naturalized citizens, rescinding their citizenship by means of what might be called denaturalization on suspicion and following up with deportation.

The show cases, such as the Ellis Island detention of Professor Germán Arciniegas, the threatened exclusion of Charlie Chaplin, later made effective, and the exclusion actions against Dick Haymes following his visit to Hawaii, are the ones that make the headlines. The more significant facts are that, through the screening procedures that have been set up, our shores are made even less hospitable than is specified by law. The resident alien and the naturalized citizen are kept in special jeopardy, especially if there is anything about their politics that smacks of nonconformity.

The close scrutiny of the political inclinations of prospective visitors and immigrants got much of its impetus from the federal employees loyalty program set up by President Truman on March 22, 1947. Traditionally the United States had gone on the assumption that its employees would be loyal Americans, and unless there was evidence to the contrary they were so regarded. The government studiously refrained from prying into their political beliefs and associations. Since 1883, in fact, the Civil Service Commission's standing rules had expressly forbidden any questioning that might disclose political or religious affiliations.

In 1939, however, the Hatch Act made it illegal for a federal employee to belong to an organization which "advocates the overthrow of our constitutional form of government in the United States." Two years later Congress forbade payments to any person "who advocates, or who is a member of an organization that advocates, the overthrow of the Government of the United States by force or violence." Neither act specifically identified the forbidden organizations, but it became the duty of the executive arm of the government to screen personnel. That was done department by department, but with an interdepartmental committee to which appeals might go. Investigation was not automatic but occurred only upon receipt of complaint or if reason seemed to exist. In the great majority of instances it did not yield evidence to justify dismissal. Some persons, however, were removed from the payroll. The Civil Service Commission also began to apply similar tests to applicants for federal jobs. Between July 1, 1940, and December 31, 1946, it dealt with 392,889 applicants and on grounds of political records adjudged disloyal, it rejected 1,307, or approximately one-third of 1 per cent.

A side effect of these dismissals and rejections was that federal employees felt inhibited from activities and associations which seemed to them innocent but which the authorities might reckon disloyal. The employing officers, too, wary of subsequent reinterpretation of these regulations, had a tendency to bypass persons whose records were at all radical. Notwithstanding these results the Republicans in Congress began to clamor for a more rigorous screening of federal personnel. It may have been partly to steal this Republican thunder that President Truman set up his more elaborate and severe program. One motive certainly was to avert legislation that probably would have been more extreme.

According to the new order any employee whose loyalty was questioned was to have a hearing before the loyalty board of his department or agency. The charges were to be made known to him, though it was recognized from the start that full disclosure would not always be possible. Evidence regarding association would be considered, and for this purpose the Attorney-General issued a list of subversive organizations, but the President explicitly asserted that the fact of membership in such an organization might or might not help the board arrive at a conclusion. Assistance of counsel was authorized but with no guaranty of the right to cross-examine or indeed any assurance that witnesses against the employee would take the stand. The department head had power to review, and his decision, like those of the regional boards that passed on charges against applicants for federal employment, was appealable to the Loyalty Review Board at Washington. This was a twenty-member panel headed by Seth M. Richardson, an eminent lawyer and a Republican.

Truman was mindful that lack of loyalty was a most serious charge. He equipped the program with a number of features designed to protect the accused, such as the partial disclosure of the charges, the right of counsel, and the review board to which appeal could be carried. Nevertheless, in these hearings, which were as momentous to the accused as a criminal trial, the agency would be both prosecutor and judge. The incriminating testimony might come from sources not disclosed to the defendant and not even known to the loyalty board. Furthermore, the criterion of decision was not held to the concrete issue of whether the accused had in any way been disloyal. The criterion was also whether he was "potentially disloyal"; it required the loyalty board and the review board to speculate on this point.

The favorite justification of this program is the dictum that government employment is a privilege, not a right. By inference then, any consideration accorded such employees is an act of grace, not something to which they are entitled. Taken literally, this doctrine would demolish the whole system of civil service and make every employee subject to instant dismissal at the caprice of the administration.

Because the details of evidence and findings are not made public, a citizen observer cannot assess the justice of this program. The grounds in some of the cases that have been publicized seem exceedingly flimsy. Guilt by association and by "sympathetic association" seem to have been carried to an extreme. The Attorney-General's list, though discountenanced in court, appears to carry inordinate weight. The Dorothy Bailey case, especially when juxtaposed with the decision on *Joint Anti-Fascist Refugee Committee* v. *McGrath*, suggests that the loyalty program accorded suspects considerably less than due process.

The program did not satisfy the politicians who kept shouting for a still more ruthless cleansing of the rolls. By reducing the government employee to subordinate citizenship, it damaged morale, especially in the policy-making echelons. These people, as Francis Biddle has said, "felt the walls close around them." The program went far toward sanctioning guilt by association and the Attorney-General's list. It stimulated similar actions at the state and local level. It set the pattern for much of the infringement of the freedoms which followed. In the light of President Truman's genuine concern for civil liberties and his sincere devotion to the freedoms, these consequences were most contradictory.

An early step of the Eisenhower administration was, again by executive order, to modify this program. Suspected subversives thenceforth would be lumped with other security risks who were merely garrulous or bibulous. Out of this arose the inflated claims of 1,456, 2,200, or 2,427 subversives removed and the later figure of 8,008. The other main change was to abolish the right of appeal beyond the department head. In most other respects the Truman program was continued. Again, the data for judging the worth of the program were not confided to the public. The few cases that have come out into the open do not inspire confidence that justice is the result.

For example, reserve officer Milo J. Radulovich was under fire because his immigrant father had received copies of certain Communist newspapers from central Europe and his married sister had attended meetings classified as Communist-front. The loyalty program ground away, and Radulovich would have been cashiered except that alert reporting by Edward R. Murrow stirred the conscience of top level administrators and brought them to the rescue. Otherwise the score would have been 2,428.

Whether Radulovich is at all typical of the persons caught up in the Eisenhower loyalty program is impossible to say. As with its predecessor, the records are not open to inspection and therefore the validity of the decisions cannot be properly judged. The queries concerning the wisdom of the Truman program apply with even greater force to the wisdom of this successor program. The unrest created in government service likewise must be proportionately greater.

Another phase of government drastically altered in recent years is the Federal Bureau of Investigation. In 1924 when Attorney-General Harlan F. Stone set the policy for this agency, he was fully conscious that a secret police could menace the institutions of freedom. He therefore specified that the FBI was not to be "concerned with political or other opinions of individuals," but on the contrary "only . . . with their conduct and then only with such conduct as is forbidden by the laws of the United States." So it continued for a decade and a half.

Then after about 1939 a series of laws and executive orders made the politics, associations, and expressed beliefs of federal employees more and more a matter of official concern. For the searching out of such data the FBI seemed the natural agency. Over the years this phase of its work was steadily enlarged. Dossier-compiling came to be its main function and by far the most publicized. The core relates to government employees, but informings on other persons were also gathered, because they applied for passports, or were considered for government appointments, or because their names cropped up in the course of investigating others. The accumulated dossiers run into the millions, and they reflect the transformation of what originally was a Federal Bureau of [Criminal] Investigation into a Federal Bureau of [Political] Investigation.

Even after this conversion, the restraints and decorum imposed by J. Edgar Hoover succeeded remarkably well in keeping the FBI out of politics. Over and over he insisted that the function of the bureau was to collect data but not to evaluate, and, at least before the public, until put on the stand by his chief in the Harry Dexter White affair in November, 1953, he maintained his reticence about passing judgment. As much as any one factor, this restraint gave the American people confidence that here was that rarest of phenomena, a secret police that was not destructive of the freedoms of the individual.

Concern, nevertheless, was sometimes expressed that the files of the FBI were a powder keg that might sometime be put to unscrupulous use. Hence the twinge of horror when a congressional demagogue or a committee employee or even a private employer claimed, and seemed to have, access to the files. Director Hoover was adamant that the files must be kept secret, in the interest of national security and to protect the bureau's informants and thus prevent the drying-up of its sources. On occasion he did add that much of the material was raw and unevaluated; and since much of it came as hearsay and some of it from vindictive talebearers, it could hardly have been otherwise. In rare instances the reliability of the FBI files and findings was questioned. An opinion poll, however, would have given and still would give this agency an almost perfect bill of health—incorruptible, impersonal, and almost infallible.

This high esteem was forcibly demonstrated in the summer of 1957. In the case of Clinton E. Jencks the Supreme Court had ruled that as defendant in a criminal case he was entitled to inspect any statements that prosecution witnesses had made to the FBI which related to their testimony in the trial. This decision merely affirmed a long-established principle regarded essential to fair trial, but it touched off a great furor. The one justice who dissented led off by conjuring up a picture of "a Roman holiday" for criminals, who now would be licensed to "rummage" through the FBI files. The Department of Justice accepted the decision "in principle," but sought immediate legislation that would protect the files and the prosecutions of alleged subversives. Stories, which some have labeled inspired, began to appear about the number of cases that would have to be quashed and the jail doors that would swing open. The editorializers enlarged and embroidered on this theme. The decision had been much narrower. It did not call for free run of the FBI files but merely that, where an FBI informant was used as a witness, the defense should be allowed to inspect whatever else he had said to the FBI that was relevant to this testimony. Congress quickly showed itself in full step with the popular clamor. In the closing days of the session, with only a token hearing and with a minimum of serious consideration, especially in the House, it rushed through a measure that was at once a rebuke to the court and a preservative of the sanctity of the FBI at the expense of one assurance of fair trial.

The sanctity thus preserved would be of the FBI as a secret gatherer of data on individual Americans and as its own evaluator and judge of such data. Therein, as should be apparent, the bureau has been at work along a line far more appropriate to a police state than to a freedom-respecting democracy. It is not just a coincidence that this change and expansion of the functions of the FBI occurred at a time marked by the fading of several of the traditional freedoms.

7. Beyond the Law

With the announced aim of containing the American Communists our government has gone to lengths ordinarily encountered only in a police state. Yet these actions, extraordinary as they have been, have not kept pace with public opinion. In consequence, resentment has flared against the majestic slowness of the law, against the red tape that often prevents quick conviction. Private citizens therefore have been tempted, individually or in organized groups, to take matters into their own hands. At their best such usurpations may prove a short cut to justice. At their worst they substitute private vengeance.

In our system it is always alarming when public sentiment and the law get out of step. One such instance is still green in our memory. On that occasion, through the Eighteenth Amendment and the Volstead Act, the law advanced to an extreme position. Public opinion, especially in the larger cities, did not go along. The result was ready tolerance for disregard of these particular laws, and then, by easy transition, came gangsterism and a general disrespect for law. Prohibition at length was repealed, but the damage lingered on.

Now on the Communist issue history has been repeating itself, but with the variation that it is the law that remains moderate while the people would rush on to more drastic experiment.

Again there is the atmosphere of unwillingness to be bound by the law, to flout it, this time by going beyond what it authorizes. Again there have been alarming side effects. Their seriousness is suggested in Judge Learned Hand's observation, "Risk for risk, for myself I had rather take my chance that some traitors will escape detection than spread abroad a spirit of general suspicion and distrust, which accepts rumor and gossip in place of undismayed and unintimidated inquiry."

One solution often proposed is to outlaw the Communist party. At a stroke, it is argued, this would harmonize the statutes with the public's righteous indignation. What is hoped for in most of these proposals is some sort of fiat that would immediately and completely put the Communist party out of existence. Clearly a party is an entity, as is a corporation, and can be made to feel the rigors of the law through fines, impounding its assets, padlocking its premises, the issuance of cease and desist orders, and other such steps. Under our system such actions must be based on laws of general application and must proceed by court order or be subject to review by a court. The controls visited on the Communist party have been many and stringent, but their essential nature has been regulatory, and they have not read the party out of existence.

Those who talk most glibly about outlawing Communism overlook the fact that a party is not something that can be sent to jail or disposed of by way of the electric chair or the gas chamber. If legislation is to put a party completely out of business, it will have to apply to the individuals who are or might become members, and it will have to impose a sufficient penalty to dissuade them from becoming or continuing as members.

Various suggestions along this line have been made. President Eisenhowever, for example, in his initial 1954 message to Congress, proposed that citizenship be taken away from all Communists. Congress did not oblige, but the statutes do impose a long list of disabilities. By legislation and executive order Communists are barred from federal employment. There are numerous state laws of similar nature. Texas toyed with the idea of making Communism a capital offense but compromised with an act setting a less extreme penalty. The Smith and McCarran Acts have given the federal government additional openings to move against Communist leaders and organizers, but as matters now stand it is not a crime, except perhaps in Texas, to be an ordinary member in this party, and except in the Lightfoot and Scales cases, no one has been convicted on this simple charge. In October, 1957, the Supreme Court set aside the Lightfoot and Scales convictions but on a subordinate ground and without deciding the issue whether membership of itself constitutes a crime.

The reasons against "outlawing the Communist party" (presumably by making mere membership a high crime) are many and compelling. Even some of the most vociferous critics probably are aware that the more extravagant charges are unsubstantiated. On the matter of the members as captives of the party, for instance, testimony and the record have established that there was a sizable turnover in membership; people came in and people went out, usually on their own volition. In the United States, furthermore, the party did not have the means of maintaining the ironclad discipline attributed to it. Some members jumped like puppets at every twitch of the party line, but this did not extend to every card-carrier and indeed was one of the reasons for the shifting membership. Again, testimony and the record indicate that Communists characteristically were so by personal conviction and not by forfeit of their intellects. In fact, the soundest criticism of them is that they are a dedicated personnel.

Certain Communists no doubt have believed as charged that Russia more than the United States is the hope of the world. Some as charged were parts of an apparatus directed from Russia. Some have been convicted for espionage and others for engaging in conspiracy. Still others have jumped bail and may have given false testimony or violated other laws. Yet as undoubtedly is apparent to our legislators, such derelictions by no means pin equivalent guilt on every Communist or indeed on the rank and file of party members.

There is something naïve or false in the incessant clamor from our lawmakers for drastic action and the studious avoidance by these same lawmakers of legislation that would achieve a surgically clean excision of this denounced minority. Such an operation would sacrifice the political capital that can be made so long as there are American Communists available for attack; some of our politicians no doubt have preferred a "dirty-bomb" attack with calculated fall-out on many non-Communists as well as on party members. Anti-Communist campaigning has had all these complexities and more.

Not least among the reasons for not outlawing the party, but likewise not greatest among them, has been J. Edgar Hoover's repeated warning that by forcing the party underground such a measure would make FBI surveillance much more difficult.

A more fundamental objection is that our philosophy of government, which forbids a bill of attainder pointed at an individual, will not permit blanketing a whole group in a legislative conviction. It is not our method to single out any class or sect or minority and reduce it to inferiority before the law. On the contrary, we insist that our laws, whatever they are, must be general in application. Thus, unless we abandon one of the major American tenets, we cannot have a law that is solely for Communists. Instead, every person in the land would have to be liable to its specifics, and, as to Communists, only those who in person violate it would be subject to conviction and sentence. On this account the remedy of "outlawing the party" has been bypassed, and wisely.

Meanwhile, not in a position to bring the law up to the fever pitch of our anger, we as a people have chosen to vent our wrath against the American Communists by going beyond the law. The government, it is true, operating within the framework of duly enacted law, has put a few score Communist leaders in jail and has eliminated known Communists from government employment. But the really massive pressure against this particular element in the United States has been administered outside of court and through processes not dignified by law.

This extralegal drive against today's hated irregulars has been likened to the way in which the pioneer West handled the problem of crime and punishment. The common method was by improvised courts, using many of the mechanics of lynch law but preferring the label of vigilante justice. This tradition, and particularly San Francisco's famous committees of 1851 and 1856, clearly are what inspired California's leading banker a few years ago to propose recruiting a modern vigilante group to take the Communists in hand. The technique continues to have strong appeal in the West; midway in the court proceedings against *Confidential* and *Whisper* one of Hollywood's leading men proposed to rally a vigilante band to put these magazines out of the scandal-mongering business.

Because they are less responsible than the regular courts, volunteer judges and avengers can deal swiftly with suspects. This is as true today as it was in frontier times. There are a number of respects, nevertheless, in which the comparison with the frontier does not hold. In their day the pioneers could assert that their impromptu tribunals were necessary because the regular codes, courts, and prisons had not arrived on the scene. They could claim, too, that the offenses for which they punished —murder, robbery, assault, and the like—were genuine crimes, universally recognized. The private prosecution current today has neither of these justifications. The regular courts stand open; and the central fact charged—membership in the Communist party—is not in and of itself a violation of the law.

The frontier vigilantes were an ad hoc committee, met to deal with one or more persons suspected of having committed a specified act of violence. The modern people's "court" is permanently in session and is concerned less with overt acts than with ideas or memberships allegedly held. The frontier tribunal consisted of a score or two or in exceptional instances of a few hundred men. The modern substitute for the regular judiciary sits nationwide. So far as they could, the pioneers simulated a real court with judge and jury, counsel for the prosecution and the defense, and designated persons to carry out the sentence rendered. In the modern style there is much less formality. True, there often are self-appointed tribunes who present the charges. There are volunteer witnesses such as the veterans at Norwalk and professional informers such as Elizabeth Bentley, Paul Crouch, and Manning Johnson. "Experts" on the philosophy of Communism, such as Whittaker Chambers, or on Communism as a conspiracy, such as Sidney Hook, are invoked. With map and pointer McCarthy did indeed lecture the television audience on the Communist apparatus. But this sort of thing did not end with McCarthy; the battery of voices for the prosecution extends ever so much further. It includes a vast array of educators, preachers, writers, editors, commentators, platform, radio, and television performers, and, above all, political orators who descant on the evils of Communism. The jury they address is spread as far as newsprint, magazines, the air waves, and the coaxial cable can reach.

In today's out-of-court "trials," furthermore, it is a matter of indifference whether the accused is present. Additional names are dropped in helter-skelter. Accusation customarily is all that is required for proof and conviction. The press release substitutes for writ and judgment, and trial by headline becomes a reality. In trial by television, democracy is mocked by the reference to "the jury of twenty million"; yet in a larger sense it is true that such trial as exists in today's direct-action purging is before the bar of public opinion. Furthermore, for carrying out the sentence the reliance is on society as executioner.

In the frontier practice of extralegal trial and punishment, the vigilantes almost invariably were private citizens. An exception so rare as to be highly newsworthy occurred in Los Angeles in 1855 when Mayor Stephen Foster took the lead in a lynch-law hanging. He was punctilious, however, about resigning his office before the vigilantes went into action and not resuming it again until that work was completed. The pioneers generally recognized that vigilante or lynch law was a competitor and a threat to regular justice. In most instances law enforcement officers wanted no part in it.

In the 1920's when the Ku Klux Klan was revived as a direct-action fraternity, this line of distinction was often forgotten, and public officials, even some in high position, became members. This fact, when it became known, heightened the general concern about the Klan as a threat to the basic institutions of the United States.

By contrast, in today's out-of-court prosecution of Communists and assorted bystanders, public officials have been among the most active participants. And, more striking, the general attitude seems to be that it is altogether proper and fitting that those who are the staff of law and order should double as the main agents in judging and punishing outside the law.

Officialdom's unofficial manhandling of Communists and others has taken a variety of forms. The waves of requiring test oaths of public employees, teachers, and persons in public housing, on relief, on state pension, or applying for tax exemptions are a case in point, though in some instances the courts have ruled that these requirements have legal sanction. Some of the library censorship moves and the more extravagant efforts to police the thinking in the schools and colleges have likewise patently exceeded the law. Denunciation of suspects is the more characteristic form, and this is something in which officials high and low have engaged, including even the nation's top law enforcement officer, the head of the Department of Justice.

In the official ranks, however, the prize exploiters of anti-Communist sentiment have been the legislative investigating committees. Theoretically in search of information as a basis for lawmaking, these committees too often seem to have quite a different purpose. Some of their hearings have been timed to have maximum effect on local or national elections or a pending labor contract or a strike. Even more often the emphasis has gone to "educating the public." Yet investigating committees are not set up to be propaganda agencies. No matter how dramatic they make their hearings, it is not their function to be a Voice to America. Nor are they licensed to usurp the role of the regular courts. Much of their "educating" and most of their efforts "to root out subversives" from government and quasi-public jobs have taken the form of exposure of suspects, which in many instances has been nothing less than character assassination.

The Army-McCarthy hearings brought this fact into full view and then illustrated it to perfection. In the colloquy about the 130 alleged Communists at work in defense plants, Counsel Joseph Welch wanted to know why their names were not reported at once to the Secretary of Defense so that "before the sun went down" they could be put out of these plants. Witness Roy Cohn scouted such an approach as too naïve. The way to do it, he said, was to subpoena these 130 as witnesses, ask them the usual questions, and, when they refused to answer, they would be stamped as "Fifth Amendment Communists" and promptly dismissed by their employers. It was as frank a statement of the kangaroo-court functioning of the McCarthy committee as anyone could have given.

A day or two later the television audience actually saw a character assassination take place. As an obvious diversionary tactic and in protest against the cross-examination to which Cohn was being subjected, McCarthy taxed Welch with trying to bring into the case as assistant counsel a man from his own firm who had a Communist-front record. The record was of membership in the National Lawyers' Guild, which McCarthy identified as cited by the Un-American Activities Committee as "the bulwark of the Communist party." The young man in question had held such a membership in his student days and for a few months thereafter. McCarthy seemed not at all impressed that he was now an active and stalwart Young Republican, esteemed and respected in his work and his community. On the basis of this one earlier association, he insisted, this man must be written off as a menace to the country and, by implication, as nefarious a character as any of the Communists McCarthy had been exposing.

Counsel Welch entered a most eloquent protest against this "reckless and cruel" charge. His answer, as perhaps it should have been, was emotional and strictly personal and addressed to the incalculable damage that was being done to this fine young man. The audience was moved to applaud. It is not recorded, however, how many there and at their television sets realized that here in epitome was the legislative investigator in his most characteristic role and his most vicious.

When they are taxed with the damages done by this kind of exposure, the committeemen offer a double excuse. Their first line of self-justification is that they are merely making known the facts, and no one, they say, should object to that. In reality, however, it often is not the truth and seldom the whole truth that they purvey. Even without an added coloring, arbitrarily selected "facts" can be completely unfair. The second excuse of the committeemen is the brazen claim that they are operating outside the law. The customary phrasing is that they are not trying anyone, much less convicting or imposing sentence. Therefore, they say, they are not obligated to observe the rituals of giving suspects the right to confront accusers, compel witnesses, or cross-examine. Technically they are not a court, but in actuality the committees have worked a condemnation on literally hundreds of persons, many of them not proven Communists, have ruined their reputations, cut them off from work and income, and left them, because of congressional immunity, with no recourse at law.

Since the penalizing is left to other hands and most of it to private employers, an accurate score on the number of persons who have suffered is impossible to develop. Some individuals unfavorably publicized by the legislative investigators have managed to hold their jobs. More have been dismissed, and the committeemen quite generally have claimed the credit. A step down from outright dismissal is the device of not re-employing, of not renewing a contract, and another step away is the device of not choosing a certain applicant for a job. In most such instances the employer or potential employer is noncommital as to his reasons, and the degree, if any, of committee responsibility cannot be determined. There is one area of employment, however, where the facts, at least in broad outline, are known, and which will serve as an example of private enforcement of beyond-the-law judgments.

In 1947, when the House Un-American Activities Committee made its first major drive to impose its particular brand of censorship upon Hollywood, the leaders in the motion-picture industry took a firm stand against the application of a political test. After the hearings of the Hollywood Ten, however, the studios did an abrupt about-face. Abandoning their former position that movie content was what mattered, they launched on a purge of Communists, persons believed to be Communists, and, by extension, persons so denigrated. On the basis primarily of the records of state and national un-American activities committees, approximately 250 writers, actors, directors, and producers were blacklisted. According to Elizabeth Poe's detailed report in the May, 1954, issue of *Frontier*, another hundred or so individuals have been "graylisted" and are equally unemployable. For some of them the derogation may have come from the committees, from the American Legion, from Hollywood's own Motion Picture Alliance for the Preservation of American Ideals, or from self-serving informers.

In an industry employing thousands, 350 persons may seem negligible. That, of course, is not the question. Where principle is involved, the statistical approach is irrelevant. We do not, for example, gloss over a kidnapping because there was only one victim. And, as Miss Poe's article goes on to itemize, the consequences in Hollywood have been much more far-reaching. A blacklist is always an open invitation to racketeering in services or supposed services for avoiding its toils or in getting whitened again and eligible to work. The fear of being summoned to clear one's self of unpredictable charges spread far beyond the 350. With it was the companion fear of not being summoned but merely dropped without any comment or explanation. Hollywood is that kind of jungle.

In any jungle the first law is to step softly. The reprisals for disapproved political beliefs and expression made many in the industry step softly. They hesitate to engage in any sort of political activity. The purge also had significant effect in undermining trade-union gains, as in the retreat on the issue of screen credits.

Furthermore, the repression has been reflected in the shying away in current picture-making from any theme or treatment that might be regarded as controversial. It is not just a coincidence that safe westerns and out-of-this-world horror stories have become the fad. Theatergoers doubtless can survive another round of Frankensteins, but meanwhile one of the most forceful channels of modern communication practically ceases to communicate. The state of mind of the picture-makers is revealed in their general unwillingness to talk about the purge and the continuing system of spying and intimidation, perhaps even to think about these things, much less to voice a protest. The pressures that have brought about this weakening of spirit are almost entirely extralegal.

The Hollywood story, though perhaps more highly colored, is of a piece with the more general pattern of this extralegal drive against Communism in America. The highlights include denunciation in much of the press, from certain pulpits, and on some of the airwaves; accusations anonymous and in the private smear sheets; swelling of the FBI and other such files with irresponsible and unverified charges; brandings through committee hearings; and privately imposed punishments. And what are the results?

One consequence is that undoubtedly a few Communists who could not have been convicted in open court have been disgraced, fired from their jobs, or otherwise penalized. On the surface it may seem that this is the way Al Capone was handled. Finding it inconvenient or perhaps impossible to convict him for the crimes of gangsterism in which it was common opinion that he had been implicated, the authorities sent him up for tax evasion. Though somewhat regretfully, we as a people are willing to tolerate punishment for something other than the main crime. If, however, the substitute charge is trumped up or a subterfuge or not even based on the law, or if the punishment is inflicted *sub rosa* rather than officially, it becomes much more difficult for the public conscience to go along with the action.

Communists, furthermore, are by no means the only victims. The aim throughout has been atrociously bad. Many persons by no stretch of the imagination to be identified with Communism have been victimized. The term "Communist" has been used most loosely. "Communist sympathizer" and "Communist thinker" are even more elastic. With these as the announced quarry, it has been possible to cut a wide swath, laying low Americans of almost every political philosophy.

Nor are the damages merely personal. Reform and liberalism in general have been intimidated. Many a liberal organization has felt it so necessary to prove that it harbors no Communists that it has had little energy left to do anything else. Many persons have hesitated to express their views on public issues for fear of being unjustly attacked. The lawless and uncontrolled character of so much of the anti-Communism now current has been largely responsible for this silencing of many voices that ought to be heard. Indeed, it may well be suspected that this effect was the major purpose of the drive as conducted.

When even a single critic is silenced, a democratic republic such as ours is hurt. When a whole wing of political and social opinion is deterred from speaking out, the danger becomes appalling. A necessary check on our government is lost, and the majority forfeits a principal aid in the study and re-evaluation of its policies.

Our preferred and tested system is that guilt is personal, that each individual is to be judged by his own acts. The crusade against Communists, particularly that part of it conducted outside the law, substitutes a judgment on the group en masse. It assumes, furthermore, that all Communists, to the letter and to the hilt, practice what their leaders preach. In human affairs, especially political, such perfection is improbable and goes contrary to reason and to experience. Mass proscription thus is unscientific.

Lawless anti-Communism also deteriorates the investigatory method. A fundamental duty of citizenship is to be a willing and truthful witness in court or before a legislative body. Yet the misuse to which the committee device has been put provokes revulsion about being a party to its punitive work. There is a civil responsibility for participation, yet on the other hand a genuine ethical barrier against being accessory in persecution. How should a subpoenaed witness resolve this conflict of moral impulses? To testify or not to testify?

The excesses of the drive against Communism have left other scars. Where we once held to the principle that a man should be deemed innocent until proved guilty, now anyone accused or suspected of being a Communist faces the uphill task of proving his innocence. Where once we deplored test oaths, we now accept them as routine. The abrasion extends to the Bill of Rights, with perceptible grinding down of freedom of speech, freedom of the press, freedom of assembly, and security against search and seizure.

Nor can anyone promise that the jettisoning of a freedom will remain on a selective basis. When a freedom declines, the far greater likelihood is that it will be lost not just for Communists, not just for government employees and for teachers, but for everybody. On such order is the price of anti-Communism carried beyond the law.

Two possible explanations exist for this resort to lawless means. One is that our feeling against the Communists among us contains something that is irrational, a senseless prejudice, an unreasoned hatred, undeserving of the dignity of the law. The other is that our system of government is equal only to the little problems and helpless when confronted by a serious emergency. The great majority of Americans almost certainly have faith in our government under the Constitution and believe further that whatever objections we have against American Communists are proper grist for the law. Indeed, the laws already on the books in all probability would prove adequate to the purpose if enforced upon the Communists and upon us all.

The lawless campaign repels because of its indiscriminate damaging of persons and reputations. It repels because of its drumhead character. It repels because so much of it is carried on by private vengeance. It repels because it substitutes guilt by association for individual trial and presumption of innocence. It repels because it silences criticism of the government and the prevailing majority. It repels on the very ground that it goes beyond the law.

8. The Decline and Fall of the Fifth Amendment

Anti-Communism as recently practiced in the United States has had numerous consequences, some of them direct and purposeful, others tangential and perhaps quite unintended. None is more striking than the corrosive effect upon the Fifth Amendment. As an integral and central feature of the Bill of Rights, this amendment was made part of the Constitution immediately after the election of the First Congress. For a century and a half it was cherished and revered. A phenomenon of the postwar years has been the sharp falling-off of popular respect for it. The drop in prestige is so marked as to suggest the possibility that this ancient prerogative may be nullified right out of the Constitution.

The Fifth Amendment is a cluster of guaranties, all concerned with the rights of the individual when confronted by the collective power of the state. It forbids seizure of property for public use without fair payment. It forbids double jeopardy. By specifying that a grand-jury indictment must be obtained before anyone can be put to trial on a major criminal charge, it protects against such action on the mere whim or malice of some official. Its central clause underlines the protective availability of the courts; no one, it asserts, shall be "deprived of life, liberty, or property, without due process of law." Along with these provisions the amendment contains a simple forthright ban against forced self-incrimination, which is now its best-known part. "No person," it says, ". . . shall be compelled in any criminal case to be a witness against himself." The courts have ruled, further, that the amendment also forbids making anyone give testimony against himself before a grand jury, a congressional committee, or other official investigations which might lead to criminal proceedings. As with much else in the Constitution the restraint is not on the states but merely on the federal government. The state constitutions, however, all contain similar provisions, some of which are older and more far-reaching than is the Fifth Amendment.

It all adds up to a reasonably complete enactment of the principle that no one shall be required to convict himself. Instead, the burden of proof is to rest upon the government as prosecutor. No one has seriously undertaken to argue against this principle as a principle. All would agree with Dean Erwin S. Griswold that "the privilege against self-incrimination is one of the great landmarks in man's struggle to make himself civilized." It is recognized as an appropriate corollary to the doctrine of presumption of innocence. But there is a marked tendency to clamor for exceptions and a considerable ingenuity in working around the prohibition.

We have this instrument as a legacy from the Founding Fathers—Washington and Madison and their associates in the Constitutional Convention and many of them in the First Congress, which submitted the amendments comprising the Bill of Rights. These first ten amendments were approved with quick unanimity. All agreed that their function was to make explicit certain principles that had been taken for granted in the original drafting of the Constitution. It is accurate to think of them as integral elements in that basic body of law.

The Americans of 1787 and 1790 in turn had this principle of barring forcible extraction of self-incriminating testimony as a heritage from England. In medieval times witnesses were forced to answer. If they were slow about it, there was no hesitancy about applying torture as a means of squeezing out a confession. This was the technique of the third degree applied in open court and by the court.

As early as the twelfth century there were protests in England about making witnesses answer. The protests seemed to be of no avail, but they continued, particularly against forcible inquiry into religious beliefs and associations. These protestants were heartened by the conviction that it was not right that the state should force them into conformity. Finally, in the 1640's the Puritans won acceptance of the principle, which ever since has prevailed in English common law, that no man shall be forced to be his own accuser.

By that time the context had come to be as much political as religious. Probes into religious beliefs and membership were still the problem, but the tie-in with political thoughts and affiliations was clear and important. Enactment of the Fifth Amendment was a direct carry-over from this Puritan achievement in seventeenth-century England. The American authors knew the menace of forced conformity, and that is precisely what they sought to ward off by means of this amendment.

For more than a century and a half the Fifth Amendment had thorough respect. Americans, both Federalist and Republican, Whig and Democrat, northern and southern, Progressive and Old Guard, New Deal and Anti–New Deal, were all for it. In public opinion, however, this respect now has only limited survival. Furthermore, the strongest popular acceptance of the Fifth Amendment is based on what seems pretty clearly to be a misconception. Today the amendment is regarded as a proper refuge for the guilty, but not for the innocent.

This interpretation has certain attractions. Yet in the eyes of the law no one is guilty until tried and convicted, by which time there is no more witnessing and no occasion to invoke the amendment. The right of refusing to testify against themselves was clearly set up for the protection of persons facing trial, either presently or at some time in the future. We know by experience that some of the persons who face the prospect of trial are innocent. We have found this to be true even among those who were suspect, accused, or indicted. Having as its first fundamental the doctrine of presumption of innocence, our system of law decrees that no one shall be treated as guilty until tried and so found. At the stage when the Fifth Amendment may be invoked, the law sees only persons presumed to be innocent, among whom a goodly number actually are innocent. Quite properly, all have equal eligibility to claim the protection of the amendment.

In the Army-McCarthy hearings Counsel Joseph N. Welch did not challenge any of the aspersions cast on the Fifth Amendment and on those who claim its privilege against self-incrimination. After the battle, however, in a reflective article he was most explicit:

"Any lawyer will tell you that the Fifth Amendment was never intended to serve as a confession of guilt. It was added to the Constitution to protect the innocent. . . . The Fifth Amendment has been resorted to . . . by many rascals, by many guilty men and doubtless there are persons invoking it today who will one day be found guilty. But no matter who invokes the amendment, it stands in our Constitution as one of the guardians of our liberties. It is for all men to use. Guilt will have to be proved in other ways, not in a way reminiscent of the medieval dungeons."

He went on to admonish: "If the phrase 'Fifth Amendment Communist' has in any way eroded your faith in the Bill of Rights, read it once again, I pray you."

The peculiar temper of our times, however, is that the plea of the Fifth Amendment is regarded as natural and proper if made by someone caught almost redhanded or against whom a great weight of evidence exists. On the contrary, if the likelihood of conviction seems remote, we are prone to say that the Fifth Amendment is out of bounds. This popular inconsistency injects a sporting attitude that is utterly inappropriate. If any selection is to be applied, it would be better morality to do just the opposite and favor those least tainted with indications of guilt.

Historically the most frequent use of the privilege against self-incrimination has been in the courts of law. Historically the most significant use has been in the area where political crimes and heresies are alleged. This privilege has been a bulwark of strength in the protection of freedom of thought and a fortunate restraint on governments sometimes tempted to prosecute for thoughts and opinions. This historical truth is one of the main reasons for Dean Griswold's reference to the Fifth Amendment as "a good friend as well as an old friend." It is also precisely the reason that was uppermost in the minds of the Founding Fathers when they added this provision to the Constitution.

Today the scene where the privilege against self-incrimination is most frequently and most dramatically invoked has shifted from the courts to the legislative investigating committees. The point at issue, however, is the familiar one of political thoughts and ideas and the attempt of the government to stamp out a particular set of beliefs and believers. As to content, therefore, this is precisely the arena for which the Fifth Amendment was designed.

Our courts, it is true, must be credited with resisting the stampede away from the Fifth Amendment. They recognize that there are unjust accusations. In almost all instances when the amendment has been invoked early enough in the questioning, and provided there is some color of possibility that a prosecution might ensue, the courts have respected the invoking of the amendment.

Theoretically, we should all be so above reproach that trouble with the law is unthinkable. Yet such is the complexity of the law today that an honest and well-meaning citizen cannot always have that high certainty, particularly if political animosity should turn its heat on him. An inadvertent breach of the income tax law is always a possibility. The Smith Act of 1940 sets up an even more formidable mantrap. One section, for example, makes it a felony, subject to as much as ten years' imprisonment and $10,000 fine "for any person knowingly to combine, conspire, or agree with any other person to perform any act which would substantially contribute to the establishment within the United States of a totalitarian dictatorship."

Several of the words and phrases in this clause are so loose and ill defined that there is no telling what they might be made to cover. Not even the present Supreme Court can say in advance what might be held a year or two hence to be a violation of this statute. Yet many an activity that was reputable a few years ago—criticizing Nationalist China, aiding refugees from Fascist Spain, or attending meetings even though a few Communists were present—is now accepted as relevant and damaging evidence. With such precedents so common, a witness altogether confident of his innocence may still need to protect himself by standing on the Fifth Amendment.

Even the least technical discussion of the Fifth Amendment must take account of two corollaries to its use. These are known as the doctrine of waiver and the no-inference rule. Both apply when the protection of the amendment is claimed in court. Waiver has been extended, perhaps inappropriately, to apply in the committee hearings. The no-inference rule, meticulously enforced in court, has not been extended to the testimony before the committees.

Waiver has to do with a series of questions so interrelated as to constitute a line. If a witness answers the first question in such a line, he is held thereby to have waived the right to invoke the Fifth Amendment with regard to any other question in that particular sequence. The burden of prophecy thus put on the witness is very great. Even a mathematician cannot find a line unless two points are given, but the witness must be able to forecast its course from only one. To preserve the right to refuse an answer to some subsequent question which might tend to incriminate him, he must refuse on the very first, which of itself is usually quite innocuous.

Experts on judicial procedure have questioned the appropriateness of the doctrine of waiver in congressional hearings. Except that it makes it difficult to force a witness to pinpoint the exact evidence which might tend to incriminate him, the doctrine is of little avail to witnesses. Unfriendly examiners use it as an excuse to berate witnesses for being unreasonably unco-operative. It also gives such examiners an opening for dozens or, if they wish, hundreds of loaded questions, on every one of which the die is already cast that the witness will have to refuse to answer on the grounds of the Fifth Amendment.

These tactics help to account for the suggestion, at present no more than academic, that the congressional committees send the doctrine of waiver back to court where it is properly applied.

In contrast, the no-inference rule is one which the committees might well borrow from the courts. A United States Supreme Court decision in 1915 stated it pithily: "If it be objected that [the defendant's] refusal to answer was an implication of crime, we answer, not necessarily in fact, not at all in theory of law." In court the impartiality of the judge is well evidenced by staunch insistence that no inference be drawn from refusal to testify. Counsel is restrained from arguing it and juries are instructed to disregard any such inference.

Our investigating committees, however, find the temptation irresistible. McCarthy set the style by branding anyone who declined to answer as a "Fifth Amendment Communist," and his mark for such a person was as black as for anyone regularly indicted, tried, and convicted. In the Army hearings, when President Eisenhower refused to permit disclosure of what went on at a top-level policy discussion, McCarthy was quick to slap back at him as a "Fifth Amendment President." In due course this catch phrase boomeranged. In presenting his bill of particulars against the junior senator from Wisconsin, Senator Flanders charged that McCarthy's many refusals to testify stamped him as a "Fifth Amendment Senator."

The habit of reading guilt into every resort to the Fifth Amendment spread far beyond the committees. The press editorialized in the same vein. Whole categories of government employees were denied its use. Private employers let it be known they would tolerate no pleaders of the amendment. The AFL-

CIO banned it for union personnel and took steps to suspend those who invoked the amendment.

The argument has also been advanced that non-resort to the amendment is proof of innocence. The Army, for example, in protesting McCarthy's allegations about Fort Monmouth, pointed out that no one at that installation took refuge behind the amendment. Instances of drawing the conclusion that refusal to testify is tantamount to confession could be multiplied endlessly, quite forgetful of the Supreme Court's rebuke, "not necessarily in fact, not at all in theory of law."

Except for the invoking of the court practice of waiver and for the disregard of the court rule of no inference—and these are exceptions of magnitude—the committees have practiced technical compliance with the Fifth Amendment. McCarthy, to be sure, erupted with periodic blasts about being sick and tired of seeing "Commies" hide behind the amendment, and Congressman Jackson was even more explicit that for the sake of the work of the House Un-American Activities Committee we must get rid of the Fifth Amendment. These statements keynoted a broader drive against this long-honored element of the Constitution.

Where this criticism arises almost without exception is on resort to the amendment before investigating committees. The officers intrusted with law enforcement are not complaining that they cannot get convictions because of the use of the amendment in court. Perhaps a culprit occasionally goes free because it is not permissible to force a confession from his mouth, but significantly it is not for the sake of what might be done in court that the clamor is raised to jettison this feature of the Constitution. The courts, it would appear, are content to continue the tested formula of presumption of innocence and prefer to leave the burden of proof upon the prosecution. Concerning the committee hearings, however, a determined twofold attack on the amendment arises.

One assault is frontal. It borrows another leaf from the procedures of the courts and proposes to authorize grants of immunity so that witnesses will be put in a position where they will have to answer. Several states already have such statutes. The immunity thus conferred holds only in the state courts, and what it will actually be worth has not been tested. A bill to authorize comparable grants of immunity to witnesses before congressional committees was passed by the Senate in 1953. Later in the year, and again with focus on the committees of Congress, Attorney-General Brownell recommended an enactment of this sort. An impasse developed over whether the discretion for granting immunity should rest with the court or with the Department of Justice. Even the weight of administration backing did not immediately persuade Congress that this device of federal immunity to witnesses before federal committees would be an improvement on the Constitution. As finally enacted in 1954, this measure provided for grants of immunity, but only when and as approved by the court.

Offhand, the immunity device seems to have the flaw of empowering government agents to shield anyone they wish from deserved punishment. For many a witness it sets up only an illusion of safety, since the complementary branch of American government is not barred from prosecuting. Offhand, it appears to be a repeal of the Fifth Amendment by subterfuge.

The other attack on the Fifth Amendment is from the rear. Because the investigating committees have put the emphasis on exposing individuals as Communists, a heavy onus of accusation rests on every witness subpoenaed. If the Fifth Amendment is invoked, the committees, though inquisitorial in character, give it technical respect. They do not take the matter to court and they do not launch contempt proceedings.

Instead, they are content to seek condemnation of the witness before the bar of public opinion. The committees usually take the lead in inferring that the refusal to testify is evidence of blackest guilt. Senator McClellan, for instance, has done so repeatedly in the course of the investigation of union leadership. The committees help spread the impression that invoking the Fifth Amendment is just another way of confessing. That is how it was done when Dave Beck of the Teamsters Union invoked the amendment rather than answer certain questions about his financial operations. The committee counsel confronted him with words from his own mouth. In 1948 when he was a regent of the University of Washington, several professors had declined to answer questions put by a committee of the state legislature. Beck read their refusal as equivalent to confession, condemned them out of hand, and urged and voted for their dismissal. In 1957 he would have liked to have it understood that it was only about Communism that refusal to testify was tantamount to confession.

This distinction was too subtle for the public generally. By this date Americans had been pretty well indoctrinated that refusal to testify was proof of guilt. Nor was that all. Use of the amendment had a further overtone, as a West Coast episode will illustrate. A ceramics company, upset by the disappearance of stray pieces of its products, brought action for theft against almost the entire work force. Since the complaints rested on little more than suspicion, counsel for the defendants advised that the simplest way to deal with the charges was for all to plead the Fifth Amendment. The men refused. Everyone, they said, would think they were Communists. Doubtless they were right—the public has been conditioned not merely to read guilt into every refusal to testify but also to think of the Fifth as the Communists' Amendment.

Thus it has come about that the ultimate debasement of the Constitution is by the people themselves. We are the ones who equate the claiming of the amendment with a plea of guilty, write off all unco-operative witnesses as Communist and unpatriotic, and sentence so many of them to unemployment and disgrace.

In 1957 a widely known philosopher set forth at book length a rationale for exactly such a turning against the historic ban on forced self-incrimination. From the standpoint of reason and morality, he says, silence must be read as prima facie evidence of guilt. He further contends that the Fifth Amendment was not needed in the 1790's and that today it is a quite unnecessary safe-guard against injustice. Although he considers it contrary to common sense, he would tolerate continuance of the practice in court, but the logical conclusion to his book should be that this part of the Constitution be discarded not just for Communists but for us all.

Some men in responsible positions rail against the Fifth Amendment as though it were a fifth wheel or an antiquated and vermiform appendage. In reality it is an essential component in our American system. If it goes, freedom of speech as guaranteed in the First Amendment will not be far behind. If it is lost, fair trial and due process of law will be very much diminished. If it is destroyed and the government empowered to crush critics and dissenting minorities, government by the people will be seriously jeopardized. Considerations such as these are worth pondering before we go any further in aiding and abetting in the downfall of the Fifth Amendment.

9. Shackling the Mind

In the gallery of José Clemente Orozco's paintings one of the most arresting is "The Slave." It is the more remarkable because no human feature is revealed, not the hands or the mouth or the eyes or any of the other elements usually thought of as most expressive. Only the head is shown. It is hooded, chained, and fastened with a great lock. And whether the hands are manacled and the ankles fettered does not matter. The bondage is complete, for shackling the mind is the ultimate in enslavement.

Purposely or otherwise, anti-Communism as practiced in the United States has involved much mind-shackling thought control. It has been, above all else, an attack upon dissent and a drive for conformity. The conformity sought, furthermore, has been primarily that of thought and belief. In the legislative investigations and in the trials under the Smith Act, for example, the reference to an overt act is seldom even nebulously present. The actual inquiry is much more to the nature of a person's convictions, his ideas, and his beliefs. It is his mind that is probed, and essentially for the purpose of protecting the American mind in general against pollution with ideas branded as dangerous.

This drive as it has operated has been in the main a matter of the emotions. Some analysis has been offered of Communist theory and program, but far more has been said in abuse of that doctrine and its adherents and in inflammatory demand that they be wiped out. The appeal is to passion, and in all this fulminating the main leverage is hate and the fulcrum on which it rests is fear.

The drive often takes leave of logic and reason. We ridicule the Russians for regimenting scholarship and requiring a party-line history, and even a party-line science. Among us the scholar is often brushed aside as visionary and impractical, and there is something of a tradition of anti-intellectualism. Nevertheless, we insist that ours is an age of enlightenment, representing the last word in scientific insight and exactitude. Therefore, before any body of thought is ruled out and its subscribers cast into outer darkness, reason must be invoked, if not actually exercised. Such an attempt has been made in behalf of the current drive for conformity; its logic, however, leaves much to be desired.

Contrary to the testimony of the experts, the idea has been popularized that our military defense hinges primarily on one or two supersecrets. The atomic bomb, when it was unleashed, did appear to be, by itself, a decisive weapon. The high secrecy that had shrouded its design and manufacture suggested a pattern that might be applied to every other phase of the defense effort. As of today, however, even with the addition of the hydrogen bomb, in which the United States had temporary lead, and the long-range missile, in which Russia has the lead, again presumably temporary, the military picture is more normal, and success is more apt to flow from the non-mysterious factors of quality and quantity of matériel and of leadership, training, and morale. Spies must be guarded against, but the major part of our defense effort is not subject to sudden disintegration through espionage.

The size, spread, and diversity of our economy and of our military likewise reduce the exposure to disaster through sabotage. Nor is it as though no precautions were being taken. And as to revolution, the American Communists are so few and so thoroughly discredited that it is preposterous to assume that there is imminent peril of the United States being taken over by this handful of "merchants of unwanted ideas."

In the methodology of American anti-Communism there are further elements of unreason. There is, for example, a proneness to jump to the conclusion of guilt. Mere accusation is accepted as proof. So is association, which at most is a form of circumstantial evidence. Such evidence, however, is arbitrarily selected, with seldom if ever an effort to consider all the circumstances, all the associations, before venturing a judgment. In the marshaling of testimony about associations, the elementary precaution of testing the reliability of the informants is repeatedly neglected. Contrary to the rules of evidence and of common sense, irresponsible, incompetent, prejudiced, self-serving, and vindictive testimony is accepted and handled as though it were the absolute truth. The public records of committee hearings are full of such testimony. The committee reports give high credulity to it. Far less has been disclosed about the content of the FBI files, but enough to create uneasiness that they also are cluttered with gossip and charges that, unless subjected to critical testing, should not be accepted as established fact.

The pall of secrecy is itself a barrier to the full exercise of reason. If the evidence is not open to inspection and rebuttal, it cannot be properly weighed and judged. In the realms of intelligence and counterintelligence we have long been accustomed to the secret gathering of data on which military and foreign policy decisions might be based. The transfer of this technique of secrecy to the domestic scene is more novel in the United States. It is plausible to argue that it may be a useful guide for lawmaking and for domestic policy decisions. But to use secret and untested evidence or privileged testimony as the basis for a verdict against an individual runs contrary to our concept of justice and contrary to reason. Yet in loyalty and security procedures this has become commonplace.

Abuse of legislative immunity likewise stands in the way of critical appraisal of testimony. For whatever he says or writes the ordinary citizen is responsible under the laws of libel. Legislators quite properly are not accountable in court for what they say on the floor of Congress. With decreasing justification this immunity spreads to remarks entered by extension of the record, to things said in committee hearings, and to quotations or paraphrases of any of the foregoing no matter where or how often repeated. The effect is that the gates are opened for unlimited accusation which is literally irresponsible. There is intellectual irresponsibility here, too, because the free-wheeling accusers do not have to come forward with proof.

In certain court decisions and in the justification of certain phases of the program of thought control, logic has been tortured. In 1952, for example, the California Supreme Court found itself in search of a formula to reconcile a newly enacted test oath with the pledge of loyalty specified in the constitution and the further enjoinder in that same section, "and no other oath shall be required." The legerdemain adopted was to say that, although the words were different, the new oath of denial was really identical with the old positive pledge. Since it was the same, the court held, it might properly be required in addition to the established oath. The court's formula ($a = b$, therefore, $a + b = a$) is both facile and fallacious.

These several indulgences in unreason are alarming enough. There is another that goes to the seat of the hysteria characteristic in America. It is the assumption that by taking sufficient precautions we can have absolute security. This illusion prompts the urge to get everybody to take an oath, to get a security check on every individual, to cloak every military preparation with full secrecy, to encourage every citizen to inform on his neighbors and every government employee to spy on other agents of government, to maintain that no one is exempt from criticism and that anyone criticized is suspect, and to put every suspect under round-the-clock surveillance. The trouble is that the machinery of all-encompassing scrutiny hamstrings more than it safeguards. It raises doubts more rapidly than it disposes of them. Aside from the direct costs, it saps initiative and lowers morale, and its purely negative approach stultifies the spirit of active devotion to American institutions and ideals.

In addition to departing from reason, today's concerted drive for security through conformity is an outright effort to suppress certain thoughts. There is a tried and tested way, of course, through which erroneous notions can be disposed of. It is to bring them out into the open market place of ideas, expose them to full scrutiny, and meet them head-on with other and better ideas. That is not the practice now being used to combat political radicalism. Instead, the modern conformists prefer to intercept contrary thoughts before they get into the open, to sandbag them, and to suppress them by force or fiat rather than vanquish them by the power of reason.

In this campaign to suppress dissent the advertised target is Communist thought. By the easiest of transitions, however, the ideas of Socialism can be included. The temptation is to go on to the New Deal, the Welfare State, the United Nations, internationalism, government ownership and controls, and so on almost ad infinitum. In short order this program becomes a very pervasive anti-intellectualism.

It attacks men of religion who engage in political or social criticism. It tries to block public speeches by controversial figures. It exerts pressure against radio or television time for voices of dissent. It tries to intimidate the press from expressing any contrary views. It goes on to outright political censorship of books and magazines and of libraries. In particular it has invaded the schools and colleges and has attempted to specify what shall be studied and taught and by whom, what conclusions shall be reached, and what thoughts and ideas shall be permitted to circulate.

Thought control as thus attempted violates freedom of religion, speech, the press, and assembly as guaranteed in the Constitution. More directly it violates another principle vital to America, a freedom less familiar and less understood, the one called academic.

If a prize were to be offered, it is doubtful that anyone could devise a less attractive name. According to the dictionary, "academic" means "theoretical and not expected to produce a practical result." In common speech it carries suggestions of pettifogging, hairsplitting, and being divorced from reality. The word is also used to denote a cold, mechanical quality, the opposite of human. "Academic" certainly is not a word to conjure with. Teachers and researchers may find it acceptable, but to the public the sound is no more endearing than if we called it "ivory-tower" freedom.

The label is made worse by the narrowed and distorted working definition often given to it. Again and again academic freedom is shrunken to a mere personal right. There is talk about the professional scholar's right to teach or to his job. Academic freedom is spoken of as something earned by so many years of good teaching or as part of the pay for teaching. Coming to regard it as a personal possession, scholars have felt at liberty to barter it away for favors or hopes of favors.

In reality, academic freedom is not so abstruse and it is by no means a privilege set up for the peculiar benefit of the professional scholar. Its simple objective is that minds be free to do their best work. It holds that there should be freedom to learn. On one level this means freedom to acquire such knowledge as others have worked out and verified. Here it touches every school child and every person in the country whose mind is still open and impressionable. For the sake of all these learners there must be freedom to teach. The ideal is that the pathways toward grasping the truth shall be kept open, that none shall be arbitrarily blockaded, and that instead of being propagandists or indoctrinators those who teach shall concentrate on helping in this reaching out toward the truth.

In addition, there must be freedom to continue the testing and winnowing of all that we and our predecessors have learned. There must be freedom, too, to pursue the truth still further and to add, if possible, to the grand total of human knowledge and wisdom. In technical language, this means that research and scientific analysis shall be unhindered. More simply it asks for honest thinking. The aim of academic freedom is that society shall be given "the truth, the whole truth, and nothing but the truth." Its symbol is the unshackled mind.

The modern American may not quite grasp the truth that "independent thought is the ultimate reliance of the race," but he is actually in pretty thorough agreement with reliance on reason and intelligence. For problem-solving he has more confidence in the force of the mind than of emotion or superstition. For most branches of science he fully accepts it. For example, in medicine, agriculture, the development of bigger and better weapons, and the devising of more ingenious gadgets, Americans are committed to unrestricted study and research. History and the social sciences often are put under superpatriotic pressure to hedge on uninhibited research and impartial teaching. Still, modern man is tough-minded. He does have respect for facts. Though not unswervingly logical, he believes in reason and has confidence in the scientific method. The thing he frequently has not grasped is that academic freedom makes possible the application of intelligence to our problems. Once aware that academic freedom does precisely that, the average person today would be much more inclined to line up in its support.

Unless it exists, we as a people are doomed to be unhistorical—to fumble at our tasks without the help that could come from knowledge of past experience. Without it, we as a people must necessarily be at least partly unintelligent—able to apply to our problems only a fraction of the brain cells that might be enlisted. Fundamentally, it is academic freedom that makes possible the application of the full mind-power of the state and nation, even of the world. It purposes that minds be permitted and encouraged to do their best work. Colloquially it is the between-the-ears freedom. Or, in terms that better express its social significance, it is freedom to learn, to think, to apply honest and accurate thought to all our problems.

In the United States there is a very special reason for supporting a freedom dedicated to the increase of knowledge, the ceaseless sifting and winnowing of the facts and generalizations presumed to have been established, and the spread of this knowledge without hindrance or distortion. For the United States, to our great good fortune, is one of those countries in which the people have the final say. In so simple a thing as an airplane no one would choose to have part of the dials and gauges blacked out from the pilot's view. In an automobile no one would choose to have the driver blindfolded. In our government the people sit in the driver's seat. By itself academic freedom cannot make all men paragons in knowledge and wisdom, but it is the factor that enables the electorate to act on the basis of knowledge and understanding.

Academic freedom in this real meaning of the term is an admirable and necessary adjunct to democracy. It is something in which every person in the country has a stake. Furthermore, it is the principle which underlies the American faith in education, to which our impressive school budgets and systems stand as monuments.

In American practice, however, academic freedom was slow in coming into recognition. So long as schooling was primarily a matter of rote learning, the inquiring mind seemed little called for. So long as advanced training was chiefly for the ministry and the law, both of which stressed orthodoxy, the concept was not likely to arise. Yet the Northwest Ordinance, initiating federal land grants for education, along with other education charters implied the principle. At the launching of the University of Virginia, Thomas Jefferson put it into clarion words. "This institution," he said, "will be based on the illimitable freedom of the human mind. For here we are not afraid to follow the truth wherever it may lead, nor to tolerate any error so long as reason is left free to combat it." In 1894 the regents of the University of Wisconsin rededicated that institution "to follow the indications of truth wherever they may lead" and to "that continued and fearless sifting and winnowing by which alone the truth can be found." In this century, particularly through the attentions of the American Association of University Professors, the principle of academic freedom has been further elaborated and particularized.

On a broader base, however, the conviction that there must be freedom for the inquiring mind has been handed down to us as a heritage from the ages. Who first recognized the need would be hard to say. But in ancient Greece Socrates for one was aware of it. The root of his trouble with his fellow Athenians was that he had stimulated his students to question accepted ideas. Asked to desist, he answered that he would not stop, he could not, and that Athens in fact should reward him for shaking the complacency and quickening the minds of its youth. The hemlock was his reward.

On another scene the Dominican friar Savonarola eloquently denounced the low estate of Florentine morals and politics. Under the spell of his words his fellow townsmen began to reform. Before long, however, the influence of the Medicis led the pope to order him to cease preaching. Savonarola resisted, and in 1498, when the Florentines turned against him, he was burned at the stake.

A generation later the king of England decreed a new orthodoxy in religion and ordered all his subjects to conform. Many looked askance at the change and at the highhanded manner in which it was made, but only two men, Bishop Fisher and Sir Thomas More, author of *Utopia*, made a real stand against the king. For their nonconformity they were beheaded.

In early New England, too, the problem arose of whether thought should be regimented or free. The Pilgrim Fathers and more especially the Puritans of the Massachusetts Bay colony had fixed ideas about religious doctrine. They envisioned a government so closely tied in with the accepted church as to amount to a theocracy. Into this society in 1631 came a brilliant, eloquent, winsome young radical, Roger Williams. His radicalism stressed complete separation of church and state, with neither coercing any person for the benefit of the other. He argued that magistrates should not punish religious offenses such as idolatry, perjury, blasphemy, and Sabbath-breaking. By challenging the company's title, which came merely from the king and not from the Indians, Williams threatened the economic status quo. For his temerity he was banished in the dead of winter and had to seek refuge with the Narragansetts.

Except for Socrates, who was engaged in what might now be recognized as teaching, it may seem odd to list any of these men —Savonarola, Fisher, More, or Williams—as contributors to the tradition of academic freedom. Others more in the main stream of scholarship and teaching could be cited, but the fact is that it has not been solely through professional schoolmen that the dignity of thought and society's vital interest in the freedom of inquiring minds have been upheld. The modern concept of academic freedom has one line of ancestry that traces back through early American schools and colleges, the little red schoolhouse where a solitary teacher labored heroically, to the European universities of the early modern and Renaissance period. It has another line of ancestry that includes all creative minds.

Today's schools and scholars, more than even they often realize, are the custodians of this heritage. Individually, of course, they are but fragile vessels in which to hold such a treasure. It happens, every now and then, by reason of economic pressure, the insecurity of their jobs, or other such considerations, that as individuals they are not able to stand firm for academic freedom. When anti-intellectualism is rampant, personal retreat or capitulation may be unavoidable. Such a surrender may be without dishonor. No individual, however, and no group of scholars has the right to barter away the principles of academic freedom, which belong to all mankind and which were bought through the heroic labors of countless scholars and sometimes through the sacrifice of their lives.

Historically there are two ways in which academic freedom has been attacked. The cruder is by direct invasion of the classroom or laboratory to forbid a certain element of study or the teaching of conclusions which, whether or not they are true, are unpalatable. This sort of interference can disrupt a research program or a school, but it is so palpably an appeal to prejudice rather than to reason that in time it is usually subject to correction. Thus after thirty years it is now presumably safe in the schools of Chicago to give England due credit and in the schools of Tennessee to present the evolutionary hypothesis.

A more sinister method of curbing academic freedom is by leaving the classroom and laboratory alone but getting rid, usually by subterfuge, of the nonconforming teacher or researcher. The present movement to safeguard the nation by quashing dissent has favored this latter course. And with great ingenuity in inventing subterfuges. In many schools the firings thus generated have made a shambles of tenure, one of the main bulwarks of academic freedom.

In practically all institutions of learning initial appointments to the faculty and research staff are on a probationary basis. Much care is exercised in selection, academic records are inspected, letters of recommendation from scholars in the field are requested, and more often than not the candidate is interviewed. Moreover, there is a trial period ranging from a year or two to as long as eight or ten years. Not all probationers are kept on, but those that are are advanced to tenure, which means that they are promised continuing appointment for life or until retirement age is reached. The assurance of tenure has proved advantageous both to the individuals and to the institutions concerned. Its primary justification is that it removes scholarship at least a step from the whims of those who might like to coerce it. Tenure is a measure of insurance that scholars and their work will be judged on their merits.

Furthermore, if there is unscholarly work in the classroom, the profession as well as the institution has means and incentive to see that it is brought up to standard. Nor is tenure irrevocable. For incompetence, gross neglect of duty, moral turpitude, or other cause convincing to his peers, a scholar may be divested of this status. These guaranties, thus, are not unreasonable. They do not ask more than a scientific determination of fitness and a scientific measure of performance. As in the other professions, it is a matter of real concern to all how any individual member of the profession is treated. It is understandable thus that the various disciplinary groups, the chemists, the mathematicians, the psychologists, and so on, have taken a keen interest in the state of academic freedom and tenure, and that the principal professional organization, the American Association of University Professors, has drawn up what amounts to a professional code with regard to the rights and obligations of scholars and institutions. The underlying purpose is that society shall reap the full benefits that intellectual freedom has to offer.

This considered program of encouraging scholars to be guided by reason and, with no other limitations, to study and work freely, open-mindedly, critically, and honestly was an inevitable target for the emotion-driven, closed-minded demand for conformity that has swept through the United States in recent years. There were preliminary forays, but the main assaults upon academic freedom began in 1948 or 1949. After that they gained momentum. The invasion is too complicated to follow in detail, but it can be illustrated by reference to a few specific phases. Throughout there was a characteristic feature: the attack seldom related to the on-the-job activity of the scholar but concerned what once would have been regarded his private life, specifically his political beliefs and ties. Through this device intellectual freedom has been badly shaken and academic tenure at many institutions reduced to a mockery.

The earliest tour de force occurred at the University of Washington. In the summer of 1948 the state legislature's Committee on Un-American Activities—a committee shortly thereafter discredited and discontinued—came to town and held hearings on the question of Communist infiltration of the university. Before this Canwell committee five members of the faculty admitted past membership in the Communist party but denied present membership. Three others refused to testify as to membership. Following the hearings, the university administration felt impelled to press charges against six of the professors, all of whom were covered by the university's rules of tenure. According to the established routine, the charges were laid before a faculty committee, which would recommend to the president, who in turn would recommend to the board of regents.

The cases were not identical. Three involved past but not present membership and what was regarded as inadequate frankness in interviews with President Raymond B. Allen. The committee recommended against dismissal and the president and the board concurred. The board did add a curious condition of "probation," which might have occasioned more comment except that the other cases were more striking.

A fourth professor, who had refused to answer certain questions of the Canwell committee, was charged in a six-point bill of particulars, including membership in the Communist party, non-responsiveness to President Allen, incompetence and dishonesty as demonstrated in his following the "party line," neglect of duty, and refusal to testify at the legislative hearing.

Four of the eleven committee members held that this professor's non-responsiveness to the president and his concealment of his views constituted substantial neglect of duty and justified dismissal. A fifth member of the committee concurred but saw added cause for dismissal in the dishonesty of following the party line. Two others, though not convinced as to technical membership, found that this particular defendant had been a most effective agent for the Communist party. On this ground as well as the others they recommended dismissal. The remaining four members of the committee did not find any of the complaints sufficiently sustained to justify dismissal. President Allen indorsed the derogatory findings, and the board ordered dismissal. In this case there was some testimony about shortcomings in the classroom and in research, but this did not obscure the fact that the dismissal hinged on the political activities and attitudes that were alleged and on the defendant's reticence about disclosing such matters to the university authorities.

The two remaining cases held the real limelight. For each a long list of charges was advanced, but when the two men opened their defense with an avowal of Communist party membership, the complaint was narrowed to this single charge and to the

146

assertion that incompetence, dishonesty, neglect of duty, and improper behavior automatically flowed from this membership. As in the old criminal syndicalism trials and in the later trials under the Smith Act, a large part of the evidence presented had to do with the nature of Communism abroad and in the United States and the asserted disciplinary control over the minds of members. Both men denied that they had been thus coerced, and no specific evidence was brought forward to indicate that there had been any adverse effect on their scholarly work.

Eight of the faculty committeemen who sat in judgment on these cases found no basis for dismissal. They wrote two reports, because five of them wanted to include an itemization of "findings" about the nature of the Communist program and to recommend a revision of the university's tenure code, whereas the other three held that neither of these actions was the immediate and proper task of the committee. The eight were agreed, however, that the case for dismissal had not been made. The other three committeemen likewise needed two reports to state their position. By independent lines of argument they came to the conclusion that membership in the Communist party in and of itself implied incompetence, dishonesty, and neglect of duty, and that dismissal was indicated.

Except for the "findings" as to the nature of Communism, part of which he incorporated into his argument, President Allen set aside the advice of the majority of eight and sided with the minority of three. He recommended dismissal, to which the regents agreed.

This particular action was precedent-shattering. Where the advice of a faculty review board has been sought, it is unusual for a president to go contrary to its recommendation. More striking, here was dismissal based solely and exclusively on membership in a political party. The customary tests of personal character, competence, and honesty in scholarship were deliberately excluded. The case offered a precedent of automatic dismissal for Communist party members.

It also gave rise to what is sometimes called the Allen formula.

It argues that the Communist party demands uncritical adherence to the party line, that thoughts as well as actions are thereby compelled, that a Communist thus forfeits his intellectual freedom and cannot qualify for the privileges of academic freedom.

The logic of this recital is exceedingly loose. It equates what Communism asks of its members with what it gets and assumes that every Communist is letter-perfect in living up to Communist doctrine. The formula also was directly contradicted by the very cases from which it was derived. It asserted that Communists because they were Communists could not be competent or have integrity in their scholarship. Yet throughout the thirteen years that these two professors had been Communists they had acquitted themselves satisfactorily. There was no move to push them out until this political issue arose. On the record which the university itself published, the evidence is that their politics was extraneous to their functioning as scholars.

In addition to the Allen formula these Washington cases offered a whole battery of precedents that might take hold in American schools and colleges. One was the indignity of putting an accused faculty member on disciplinary probation as is done to students for misbehavior. Fortunately, this example has not been followed. A second precedent was the one directly sponsored by the Allen formula, of automatic dismissal for Communist party members. Curiously, however, this example has not taken hold either. In all the turmoil in the academic world after the winter of 1948–49, when these six cases were wound up, whereas hundreds of teachers and researchers have been thrown out, in not a single instance has the reason assigned been: You are a Communist, therefore you are fired.

Instead, the purge that has swept through the nation's academic ranks has taken its cue from the other, less-noticed precedent set in Washington. Practically every such dismissal has been grounded on the scholar's failure or refusal to respond through an oath or an interrogation to questions about his past or present political affiliations and beliefs. This device has been almost universal.

In retrospect it is hard to understand why scholars in general took so little notice of what was going on at Washington. One good reason is that through all the preliminary stages, the proper safeguards seemed to be present. The faculty review board was counted on to be fair, and it was assumed that its recommendations would carry great weight. In December, 1948, when the historians of the western states and provinces met in convention on the Washington campus, the impression gathered was that nothing untoward would happen. The president's recommendation and the board's action less than a month later came as a surprise. The complexity and verbosity of the committee findings blurred the picture and left some room for argument about the issues involved. Unfortunately, too, although the American Association of University Professors was requested to make an investigation, seven years elapsed before it issued a report and then its action was merely belatedly to deplore what had happened. In addition, many other crises had crowded into the spotlight.

Two months after the Washington regents had made their historic decision, the regents of the University of California voted to require a test oath of the faculty and employees of this largest of American universities. The action was taken in executive session and was not immediately announced; indeed, there were official denials that there was to be any such requirement. At the close of the semester, however, the oath was unveiled and the faculty had a chance to inspect it. In response to criticism it was modified and then put into the mail to each member of the staff. Through the summer the official pretense was that this oath denying Communist membership was requested but not required. It soon became evident, however, that the only way to get a contract was to sign the oath. By September, when the faculty reassembled on the several campuses of the university, about half had so sworn. There was, however, virtually unanimous support for resolutions calling on the regents to rescind the oath requirement as an unscientific and inappropriate test for membership in the faculty and destructive of the intellectual freedom which an institution of learning must have.

The controversy was at white heat through the academic year. It brought about a thorough airing of the concept of academic freedom. In personal statements and in group resolutions scholars all over the world spoke out against the political test as ruinous to academic freedom. The California faculty reiterated its stand, but in March, 1950, it abandoned the basic principle by adopting a resolution reciting the litany that proved members of the Communist party, having commitments contrary to true scholarship, are not acceptable in a faculty. To some the word "proved" was salve to conscience. But the major argument for this resolution was that the regents, it was said, would be satisfied with it and would not press for individual signatures. The remaining non-signers, it was thought, would not be fired.

The regents did convert the oath into a contractual declaration. For those not willing to make such a declaration they set up the alternative of a hearing before a faculty committee, from which could issue recommendations to the president and the regents. But when it came to a showdown, the regents refused to accept any clearances from this committee or to let anyone remain on the faculty unless he signed his personal political disclaimer. In July and August, 1950, the thirty-two professors who ultimately relied on the committee reports were summarily dismissed.

The following April the Third District Court ruled that the regents' oath-declaration requirement was unlawful, and in October, 1952, the California Supreme Court corroborated this decision. The regents, meanwhile, had dismantled their special "loyalty" requirement, substituting a more general one enacted by the legislature. With the spring semester of 1953 they did permit such of the dismissees as were available to return to their posts. A majority of the board, however, was not willing to make any payment on the salaries lost during the thirty months of unlawful exclusion from the faculty or to make good on the solemn promise of as much as a year's severance pay to those who would resign. The aggrieved professors had to sue the regents again. Late in the winter of 1954, after resisting with every legal technicality, the regents at length settled in full and with interest with the six who had resigned, but not with the sixteen who had resumed their posts. Among other arguments advanced, the attorney for the regents contended that in the University of California tenure affords no basis for a claim to continuing employment and compensation. At long last, in March, 1956, these suits were settled out of court with salary equivalents less certain offsets and with restoration of retirement and other benefits.

This California resistance is sometimes credited with preventing a nationwide epidemic of test oaths for teachers. It certainly prompted awareness of academic freedom and alerted scholars to the need for staunch defense. Also, the favorable decision gained at court stands out in bold relief against what was almost a pattern of judicial surrender of civil liberties. Yet in the university the so-called Year of the Oath stretched out to six and seven during which many of the uncertainties were unresolved, including the important question of tenure. In April, 1956, after a review of the seven-year record yielded insufficient evidence that proper conditions of academic freedom and tenure had been restored, the American Association of University Professors put the University of California on its censure list.

Meanwhile, though most often as a general requirement upon all public employees, the device of the oath of denial has been spreading. In most instances the courts have held such measures constitutional. An exception was Oklahoma's oath, enacted in 1950, which went to an extreme in applying the unalloyed test of guilt by association. A group of professors, concerned in part because of the invasion of the freedom of scholarship, exposed themselves to its penalties and tested it in court. In 1952 they were rewarded with a unanimous decision by the United States Supreme Court that the oath requirement in its indiscriminate classification of innocent with knowing activity and its total reliance on guilt by association offended due process and was invalid. This decision, warming though it was, did not bring about immediate restitution to the professors in question. They had to institute another round of litigation in the state courts which dragged on for several years.

Nor did the invalidating of the Oklahoma procedure rescind the 6 to 3 approval that the court had given a few weeks earlier to New York's Feinberg Act. This law, enacted in 1949, empowered the state Board of Regents, after notice and hearings, to designate organizations which in the board's opinion were committed to the overthrow of the government by violence. By the law and the rules of the board in pursuance thereof membership in any such listed organization would be prima facie evidence of unfitness. This evidence was not irrefutable, but if not refuted would be sufficient for dismissal. By the setup, furthermore, a hearing accorded a teacher would give him an opportunity to try to disprove an alleged membership but not to reopen the question of the subversiveness of the listed organization.

Before the board had proceeded to the point of dismissing anyone, an interested group of teachers, parents, and taxpayers took the matter to court and the Supreme Court accepted the case on appeal. The litigants had standing and, in the language of the law, the issue was "ripe." Nevertheless, the record that went forward on the appeal concerned potential rather than specific effects—no one had as yet been proved to be a member—and the court has been criticized because it "exhausted its function" on "so abstract a record."

The majority opinion suggests that the court was the more ready to approve the law because of its specific application to the schools, a "sensitive area." The phrase seems to have been carried over from its more customary application to defense secrets. The majority also noted that "from time immemorial, one's reputation has been determined in part [emphasis added] by the company he keeps." In the decision the court appeared to be prepared to let reputations be determined entirely by the company kept. This, however, may overstate the case; the abstractness of the record makes it difficult to know just how much room for rebuttal the court expected the teacher to be given. One feature entirely lacking was insistence on knowing membership—"knowing" in the sense of the member knowing that the organization in question was committed to the violent overthrow of the government. This is a conspicuous omission because in the Oklahoma oath case a few weeks later and in 1957 in certain Smith Act cases the court made this particular feature decisive.

As often happens, the dissenting opinions were far more eloquent and far more idealistic. Douglas castigated the law as based on the principle of guilt by association, which is repugnant to our society. He protested that the individual teacher in most instances would be condemned at a hearing in which he had no part and that the only defense remaining, that of establishing innocence through ignorance, was awkward and almost impossible. He saw the law not only as a curtailment of freedom of association but as certain "to raise havoc with academic freedom."

Another section of the New York law requires the removal of a teacher for any "treasonable or seditious" words or acts. Treason is explicit enough, but "treasonable words" and "seditious words and acts" are terminology open to a wide range of definition and sufficient to discourage freedom of thought and speech in an area where such liberties are of particular need and significance. It would have been interesting and important to have had this part of the law before the court. But the issue was not raised in *Adler v. The Board of Regents*; the court did not pass on it then and has not since.

Under the mandate given in the Adler decision, the New York Board of Regents has applied the Feinberg Law with the result that scores of teachers in the public schools and colleges of the state have been dismissed. Against the over-all background of the court's decision it probably can be theorized that the procedure permits much other evidence to be brought into consideration and that membership in an organization that has been classified as subversive does not necessarily stand alone as the ground for dismissal. Practice, it would appear, has often departed from theory, and dismissals have occurred with nothing in evidence other than membership. At best this is a method whereby Communists and other assertedly disloyal persons can be ousted without the necessity of presenting personal proof. It is legitimate to ask how good this best is. As the New York Times pointed out, the technique is that of the blunderbuss and has the inaccuracy that goes with scattergun blasts.

An even simpler device for weeding out suspects from the teaching profession was signed into law in California in the summer of 1953 by Governor Warren just before he left to be Chief Justice of the United States. It empowers school boards to summon teachers for questioning in five fairly broad areas and to dismiss for any failure to respond. Under this provision the state board promptly dismissed a professor from San Diego State College, the local board dismissed another at Orange Coast College, and the Los Angeles school board dismissed ten or a dozen of its teachers, announcing meanwhile that it had a list of about 170 to work through. In all instances the boards were scrupulous to assert that the dismissals were for insubordination and that no charge of Communism was made. Yet the popular reception of the news has been in the vein, "You don't want a Communist teaching your children, do you?"

Ingenious as they are, these methods are overshadowed by the interrogatories of the congressional and legislative committees. The committees provided much of the impetus. A visit by the Canwell committee touched off the Univeristy of Washington action, the specter of the Tenney committee was in the background of the California oath, and so on throughout. The committees led in developing the techniques of questioning and they are still at hand to practice it. Among schoolmen and scholars, as elsewhere in our society, it is the possibility of grilling and publicity at the hands of the ruthless committeemen that gives strength to these other devices for enforcing political conformity.

Throughout all these variants there are two criteria which are accepted as all-sufficient. One is association. To be a member of or even to mingle with and spend time with—this is proof enough of what one believes, has done, or will do. The other is unresponsiveness. In the context, "unco-operative" and "unfriendly" are the standard words. Should the witness-suspect be unresponsive, his associational errors are regarded as established.

The committeemen, it will be remembered, are specialists. They flush out, they expose, they may denounce, but punishment is something that they leave to employers and to the public. Accordingly when they turn up teachers and researchers who have had off-center associations or who are unresponsive, it is left to the respective schools and colleges to take actual steps.

Institutional reaction has varied. Some school administrators have been as incontinent as Hollywood to get rid immediately of any person thus fingered. Others have moved at more ordered pace, and still others have been unwilling to dismiss on grounds of association or unresponsiveness and nothing more.

Both terms, it should be noted, have considerable breadth. Association may be of the present, the recent past, or the remote past. It may range from most active membership to a single feather-like touch. The groups with which associations have been alleged represent a great diversity too, some being at least 99.44 per cent pure.

Unresponsiveness, likewise, can range from complete to strictly limited. Sometimes it has been confined to an unwillingness to inform on others, again to a defense of the right of privacy, a protest against an out-of-line committee, an effort to keep scholarship free from politics, a balking at irrelevancies, or a determination not to let a constitutional guaranty lapse. The crux of the matter usually has been unresponsiveness regarding past or present membership in the Communist party and, though not always explicitly, the grounding of this refusal on the Fifth Amendment.

The problem as usually stated is whether present membership or possibly just past membership in the Communist party is full and sufficient basis for exclusion from the company of scholars.

Theoretically that is the problem. In point of fact, however, the way in which it arises in academic circles is on the score of whether failure to deny such membership wherever and as often as asked constitutes full and sufficient basis for such exclusion. In practice then the question faced is a double one: Is silence an infallible proof of membership, and is membership an infallible proof of unfitness?

To this compound question two diametrically opposed answers have been given. One school of thought is represented by the American Association of University Professors, the late Robert A. Taft, Robert M. Hutchins, James B. Conant, and Nathan M. Pusey. The American Association of University Professors has long maintained the position that scholars should be judged by their individually demonstrated fitness and performance as scholars. Alert to the need for dependable tenure as a condition for academic freedom, it opposes dismissals that are arbitrary, based solely on the circumstantial evidence of association, or in which no violation of law is established.

"As a member of the board of trustees of a university," said Senator Taft, "I would not favor firing anyone simply for being a Communist unless I was certain he was teaching Communism or having some effect on the development of the students."

"I cannot insist too strongly," writes Hutchins, "that the primary question in every case is what is this individual man himself, not what are the beliefs and activities of his relatives, associates, and acquaintances."

In his final report to the Board of Overseers of Harvard University, President Conant wrote, "There are no known adherents to the Communist Party on our staff, and I do not believe there are any disguised Communists either. But even if there were, the damage that would be done to the spirit of the academic community by an investigation by the university aimed at finding a crypto-Communist would be far greater than any conceivable harm such a person might do."

His successor, Nathan M. Pusey, while making clear that Harvard did not advocate use of the Fifth Amendment, was equally emphatic that neither did it "regard the use of this constitutional safeguard a confession of guilt." Despite Senator McCarthy's enraged protests, this policy prevailed in the retention of physicist Wendell N. Furry even though he had refused answers to a number of questions posed by the Jenner committee.

There is another school of thought which favors instantaneous dismissal of Communists from scholarly posts and indorses the doctrine of guilt by silence. This doctrine has been put into practice far and wide—for example, at Boston University, New York University, the University of Kansas City, and the University of Michigan.

The dialectics of this school of thought have been repeatedly voiced. The most elaborate formalization was issued in the spring of 1953 by an organization known as the American Association of Universities. The AAU consists of some thirty-seven school heads and is not to be confused with the AAUP, the American Association of University Professors, with its some forty thousand members. The important distinction is that the AAU represents the administrative viewpoint.

Its statement discourses at length on how a university must encourage pursuit of knowledge, must permit the assertion of truths whether popular or not, and must allow for the voicing of honest opinion even when it is in error. There is a reminder, perhaps gratuitous, that except in the field of his specialization the professor is a layman and might well cultivate humility. The point is also stressed that, in the eyes of the law, scholars are on a par with other citizens, entitled to no special privileges.

On the score that the professor has prestige as an expert and as a member of a university and that by virtue of his profession he owes the public complete candor, the argument follows that, even if the Fifth Amendment is available for others, he must not claim it. To do so "places upon a professor a heavy burden of proof of his fitness to hold a teaching position and lays upon a university an obligation to re-examine his qualifications for membership in its society."

Whether or not it is so intended, the "complete candor" that the presidents demand would thrust scholars into a second-class citizenship. It would invade their privacy on matters not necessarily relevant to the discharge of their professional duties. And it would strip away a right of self-defense recognized at court.

The dogma of the presidents is even more point blank that membership in the Communist party "extinguishes the right to a university position" and that an instructor who follows "Communistic practice" by becoming a propagandist or by adopting the party line "forfeits not only all university support but his right to membership in the university."

These sentiments immediately follow a paragraph whose tone is set by the assertion, "We condemn every form of totalitarianism." Mass proscription of Communists undoubtedly has great popular appeal in the United States today, and out-of-hand condemnation of all who might be called fellow travelers will get almost as much applause. But does that make the fiat less authoritarian? And is authoritarianism consonant with the atmosphere of freedom that the presidents say a university must have, or with their warning that "to enjoin uniformity of outlook upon a university faculty would put a stop to learning at its source"?

Several school administrators have made personal statements echoing or enlarging upon the AAU refrain. These sentiments have had other expression, too, for example in the advice broadcast to the American people to be "vigilant day and night to make sure they don't have Communists teaching the sons and daughters of America." The speaker was Senator McCarthy, who went on to say that "there is no academic freedom where a Communist is concerned. He is not a free agent. He has no freedom of thought, no freedom of expression." "I don't care," he continued, "how much of a screw-ball, or a crack-pot, any professor or teacher may be as long as he or she is a free agent. But once—once you have this United States, from the Atlantic to the Pacific, covered with a network—a network of professors and teachers who are getting their orders from Moscow, from an organization that wants to destroy this nation, that wants to corrupt the minds of youth, then, Mr. Jenkins, we are rapidly losing the battle. So I would say this, the thing the American people can do is watch what's going on. . . . If they will keep a wide-open eye day and night on all of their schools, all the colleges, all the universities, and when they get information which indicates that someone is actually a member of this Communist conspiracy, send that in to our F.B.I."

A substantial drift has occurred from that first indulgence when the position was that academic freedom should be inviolate except that actual Communists were to be eliminated. Before long any scholar who at any time and for any reason refused to deny that he was a Communist was subject to equally quick dismissal, notwithstanding the Fifth Amendment. Another short step spread the ban to fellow travelers, so called, and to the still more amorphous category of "members in the Communist conspiracy." Nor is this the limit. To deal with the "controversial" is regarded as perilous and in many instances has proved so.

Clearly, several forces have combined to produce this result, but the first cause can be identified as that hasty generalization that all Communists have enslaved minds. Even if this is almost always true, the practice of expelling scholars just on the basis of the label is an unscientific short cut, a dangerous precedent, and an opening wedge for other invasions of freedom. It would have taken very little longer to have measured the actual fitness and performance of each of these scholars whose eligibility was questioned.

This broadened purge removed several score scholars from their work and income, in many instances demonstrably without adequate justification. Without minimizing the personal disaster to these people who were fired, it still may be said that they are but a small fraction of 1 per cent of the grand total of professional scholars. The consequence, however, is that fear has stalked the classroom and the laboratory. The vagueness in the charges opens the door wide. There is no telling what topic or opinion will be the next addition to the list of things "controversial"; before the 1954 overturn in Guatemala, for example, one would have assumed that revolution in the Western

Hemisphere was not something to praise or encourage. There is no telling who will be the next scholar subjected to attack.

To some extent the intimidation of scholars can be documented. In Atlantic City at the 1953 convention of the National Education Association the school superintendent of San Francisco protested that he had not come all that distance to be told that there was no threat to academic freedom. The 1954 convention was keynoted by a committee report based on information from 522 school systems. It asserted that fear was indeed widespread and that it was fossilizing education and making it sterile. It should have been axiomatic that fear of reprisal would lead to ultracautiousness and that with the decline of job security or tenure, academic freedom would also be reduced.

Undoubtedly the most spectacular example of the fear-dictated curtailment of scholarship is the cancellation of J. Robert Oppenheimer's security clearance. At the instance of Lewis L. Strauss, the head of the Atomic Energy Commission, President Eisenhower in December, 1953, suspended Oppenheimer's clearance and ordered "a blank wall" erected between him and atomic secrets. Resignation without any fanfare of publicity was suggested, but Oppenheimer, not wanting to have his character forever clouded, asked for a weighing of the evidence by the Personnel Security Board. When its report was adverse, 2 to 1, he appealed to the AEC, which held against him, 4 to 1.

Thus we had the spectacle of the directing genius of the atomic bomb, after fifteen years of superlative service in the innermost sanctum of our defense effort, suddenly rejected.

What with the complaint as originally served, Oppenheimer's detailed answer, the released testimony of many scientist-witnesses, the Gray report filed by Gordon Gray and Thomas E. Morgan of the Security Board, the dissent by physicist Ward V. Evans, the group report and individual opinions from Admiral Strauss and the businessmen who made up the AEC majority, and the dissenting opinion by physicist Henry De Wolf Smyth, the documentation is long. It also is complicated. Gray and Morgan were emphatic that Oppenheimer's actions had been unswervingly loyal. They were disturbed that he argued against embarking on the expensive and uncertain project that led to the hydrogen bomb. They opined that enthusiasm on his part might have hastened its achievement. Primarily, however, the Gray report expressed concern about Oppenheimer's former associations with Communists and his recent associations with ex-Communists. Oppenheimer's sensitiveness, which led to twinges of remorse for having helped expose the world to so monstrous a weapon, was also a factor to Gray and Morgan, but it was primarily on the basis of his associations that they reached their verdict that he was a security risk. To bolster its findings the Gray report elaborated on what it called "the jurisprudence of security," the essence of which was that doubt must be resolved in favor of the national interest rather than the individual. Scientist Evans was more impressed with the solid record of Oppenheimer's loyalty and his steadfast protecting of all the secrets, and they were many and great, that had been intrusted to him. On this basis of fact, he indorsed Oppenheimer for continued clearance.

Influenced perhaps by the press reaction against the argument that Oppenheimer had not been entitled to express his objections to the all-out effort to develop the hydrogen bomb, the AEC in effect dropped that charge. Scientist Smyth agreed with the clear conclusion of the Gray report on Oppenheimer's complete loyalty and, on grounds much the same as Scientist Evans', indorsed him as one in whose hands the highest secrets would be safe. Strauss and two of his colleagues agreed on Oppenheimer's loyalty but detected "fundamental defects in his character" and Communist associations that "extended far beyond the tolerable limits of prudence and self-restraint." One of these commissioners, Joseph Campbell, added a footnote that in the light of the developed staff of atomic scientists Oppenheimer had become expendable. Commisisoner Thomas E. Murray concurred in the verdict that it would jeopardize security to permit Oppenheimer to have access to classified data. He also condemned him for failing to show "exact fidelity" and "obedience" to established security regulations and on that ground found him disloyal.

Oppenheimer is out. Except for the Murray opinion he might seem to have been fully exonerated as to loyalty. Where this issue is raised, however, there is no such thing as complete exoneration. Moreover, the majority findings against security clearance inevitably cast some reflection on loyalty as well, and as he went back to private life Oppenheimer must have wondered just how loyal did the others who voted against him think he was. For the nation as a whole it must be disquieting that the two examiners who were most addicted to letting the facts speak for themselves and to arriving at conclusions by cold reason and logic—the two scientists—upheld Oppenheimer as to security as well as loyalty.

By most Americans the Oppenheimer case will be viewed as an isolated event. It will lead others to re-evaluate the whole of what Gray called "the jurisprudence of security." Another potential should be remarked. In its concentration on the circumstantial evidence of associations, on incidental episodes that were less than trivial in the full record of Oppenheimer's work, and occasional instances of unresponsiveness on his part, the inquiry was typical of standard procedures in the purge of scholarship. It also ran true to form in its charges of insubordination and in its alarm about the individualism of opinion that he sometimes expressed.

Emily Dickinson characterized this attitude with infinite scorn in her lines

> Assent, and you are sane;
> Demur,—you're straightway dangerous
> And handled with a chain.

Because of his eminence, the drama and perhaps the poignancy are increased, but in essence the excommunication of J. Robert Oppenheimer is a fair example of the current onslaught on intellectual freedom.

When the Soviet satellite-makers won the race to outer space and in the process displayed their substantial superiority in long-range missiles, the immediate reaction was to urge more appropriations for science. It was also said, though not so loudly, that if we were serious about wanting more and better scientific achievement we should accord our scientists more freedom. Herblock drew a cartoon of our missile and satellite program as a potted plant almost dead because its custodian had kept it in a steel safe. The restrictions on free exchange of information among our scientists came in for special criticism. Drew Pearson listed a number of top-flight research men who have been excluded from defense projects and some of them from any kind of work in science.

Again, Oppenheimer stands as something more than the symbol. After Sputnik former Assistant Secretary of Defense Trevor Gardner urged that the administration reconsider the walling-off of Oppenheimer at Princeton. Perhaps eventually he will be invited to function again under the auspices of the government, but thus far no word or action at headquarters indicates that the freeing of scientists is to extend this far.

10. The Stand for Freedom

With a few possible exceptions the leaders in the recent onslaughts on the freedoms have been men of action rather than philosophers. They are opportunists and as such are uncomfortable when asked to take the long view. It is devastating to compare them with the statesmen who established this nation; yet it is the handiwork of Washington and his colleagues that they challenge in today's drive for conformity.

These direct actionists, nevertheless, have real power. They argue, first, that the very survival of our civilization is at stake, and with the conjunction of the Frankenstein of Communist Russia and the nightmare of holocaustal weapons, that may well be so. With less logic, but persuasively, they also argue that to save our civilization we must set aside some of the traditional freedoms. On this proposition there has been no clear-cut referendum, but many evidences indicate that it has the support of public opinion.

Consequently, to be a partisan of the freedoms entails genuine risk. It is a familiar concept that freedom is seldom free, that it must be bought with a price. In the United States, however, we had come to have the comfortable feeling that the heroes of the Revolutionary generation had won these rights for us and bequeathed them to us to enjoy. Even though Jefferson warned that eternal vigilance would be necessary, it comes as something of a shock that the freedoms are a legacy that requires our perpetual care. It is still more of a shock that to be a champion of freedom of religion, of speech, of the press, or of assembly, or an advocate of due process or equality before the law exposes one to criticism as a menace to society and un-American.

Notwithstanding the weight of this antagonism, there are those who speak up for freedom. It occurs in the day-to-day reporting of the news, in the press and on the air. In that cacophony, support of the freedoms is regarded as less newsworthy than charges of treason in the Treasury Department or too much truth and not enough propaganda in the Voice of America. Such alarums have greater headline appeal and get more volume. Nevertheless, anyone who reads enough papers or turns enough dials will find reports on freedom's defense. The distribution may be spotty. For example, on the California oath controversy only one or two local papers did as good a job of reporting as did the faraway New York press.

Random voices have protested particular attacks. Thus, the Chicago *Tribune* once observed, "Senator McCarthy will better serve his cause if he learns to distinguish the role of investigator from that of avenging angel." The Los Angeles *Times* took issue with the Attorney-General's proposal that wiretapping be legalized and held that there was something to be said for the Fourth Amendment. The *Wall Street Journal* saw an element of breach of contract in the move to cancel Alger Hiss's eligibility for a pension. Edward R. Murrow did a revealing telecast on the difficulties of the American Civil Liberties Union in finding a meeting place in Indianapolis. And after the Dave Beck performance, Eric Sevareid followed the President's tremulo on the Fifth Amendment with the sage reminder that this amendment was still part of the Constitution and that it had been put there expressly to prevent wringing from any individual testimony that would incriminate him.

Another robust example is the editorial "Six Men Amend the Constitution," with which the St. Louis *Post-Dispatch* in June,

1951, greeted the Supreme Court's decision upholding convictions under the Smith Act. "There is no greater right in all the world," this editorial began, "than the right to hold free opinions and to express them without fear of reprisal by those in authority. This right is the very heart of American democracy. Keep it secure and the free way of life will survive. Take it away and the free way of life will die within itself." Yet this decision, the editorial went on to say, was an unprecedented restriction on the right to hold opinions and to express them and "the gravest departure from the guarantee of freedom of speech in our history."

When the House Committee on Un-American Activities was casting its eyes churchward, there were vigorous protests from the pulpit. In Washington Dean Francis B. Sayre, Jr., and Rev. A. Powell Davies spoke out most eloquently. Later, with more particular reference to McCarthy, Bishop Bernard J. Sheil of Chicago added a Roman Catholic voice to the protest. In an unrecorded number of other churches other clergymen addressed themselves to the same theme, with much less fanfare of publicity, but not necessarily with less effect. The Presbyterian encyclical, more elaborate and more detailed, went to that entire denomination and beyond. It is noteworthy for its content, and also because the times seemed to call for its issuance.

At a time when censorship threatened to become epidemic, the American Library Association and the American Book Publishers Council issued a ringing declaration, *Freedom To Read*. Against the current of attempts at suppression and pressures for conformity, these groups flatly asserted that "free communication is essential to the preservation of a free society and a creative culture." They concluded, "We do not state these propositions in the comfortable belief that what people read is unimportant. We believe rather that what people read is deeply important; that ideas can be dangerous; but that the suppression of ideas is fatal to a democratic society. Freedom itself is a dangerous way of life, but it is ours."

Other professional groups have had something to say about

the freedoms, usually in response to a slur on their particular fraternity. Thus the bar association in California lobbied against a special loyalty oath for lawyers and in 1957 protested a blatant disregard of counsel's rights in a Los Angeles performance by the House Un-American Activities Committee. The scholarly associations protested inroads on academic freedom. The associated scientists rallied in support of Condon, and all but a handful of the atomic scientists challenged the allegations and the procedures under which Oppenheimer was deprived of clearance.

The usual pattern is each to his own. Much more rarely clergymen show concern about freedom of political assembly, librarians support freedom of speech, businessmen indorse academic freedom, and professors rally to preserve freedom of religion. Such crossovers ought to be common. They occurred in greatest volume when the issue was joined on desegregation in the South—a civil rights issue but one interlocking with the whole cluster of civil liberties. In practical fact the freedoms are so closely interconnected that a weakening of one soon becomes a weakening of the others, and an integrated general defense is by all odds the most logical. That, however, has not been the usual practice.

At times in the past, poets and novelists spoke with great effectiveness on vital issues. The present crisis has touched few such sparks. The ballad writers also pass it by, even those who affect the calypso form, tailor-made for comment on current events. Save for an occasional excursion into history as in Arthur Miller's *The Crucible* and Jerome Lawrence and Robert E. Lee's *Inherit the Wind*, most playwrights have been busy with other themes. And with rare exception such as *High Noon*, the saga of a community's failure in the face of an emergency, the dramatists of the movies, radio, and television sedulously avoid the controversial.

In book, article, and essay a doughty phalanx of serious writers have addressed themselves to facets of the problem or to the general plight of the freedoms. The book list at the back of this volume starts such a roll call, and other distinguished names could be added, especially as contributors to the periodicals. Only one book in this list attained anything like the proportions of a best-seller, and the essays and articles, almost without exception, appeared in magazines of moderate to small circulation. The sense and wisdom assembled in these writings deserve more communication, and in other forms perhaps have had it indirectly.

For example, in the issues of the *Reporter*, sometimes with parody and always with irony, "Sec" chides those who would abandon freedom, as in his lines entitled "Insomnia":

> Count the small liberties as they leap over the stile and disappear, One by one—
> One To Differ (those who believe in other ways betray)
> Two, To Listen (this lecture is canceled; the thoughts might lead astray)
> Three, To See (this movie is banned because some call it obscene)
> Four, To Enter (this man cannot immigrate, he erred at eighteen)
> Five, To Read (these books are no longer permitted on the shelves)
> Six, To Be Silent (those who refuse to speak convict themselves)
> Seven, To Question (this judge who consulted his conscience must be impeached)
> Eight, nine, ten, eleven, twelve (the limit is not yet reached)
> Count the small liberties as they leap over the stile and disappear, One by one.

The art of burlesque has also been invoked, as in Edwin A. Rothschild's "Anti-Horse-Thief Act of 1953," to which one wit proposed a "rider" promising proper rewards and honors for the reformed horse thief; and Arthur Miller's "A Modest Proposal for Pacification of the Public Temper," the gist of which was that every American, as a gesture of civic service, should go to jail.

It may well be, however, that the palm for eloquence in freedom's behalf should go to the cartoonists. The pomposity of the congressional investigator is an ideal target for Lichty's *Grin and Bear It.* In a single panorama Fitzpatrick of the St. Louis *Post-Dispatch* epitomized the sordid and sinister in the Army-McCarthy hearings. There are a number of others but none more persistent or more telling than Herblock of the Washington *Post.* Again and again over the past several years he has acidly etched his comments on the traducers of freedom. An early cartoon captioned "Fire" showed a helmeted McCarthy scaling a ladder up the Statue of Liberty to douse the torch of freedom. Another sketched a Rube Goldberg machine for separating security risks and non-risks; with equal indignity it dumped job applicants into the hoppers marked "in" and "out." Still another, "High Noon in Washington," had Senator Knowland refusing a badge from Sheriff Flanders, while other prospective possemen disappeared in all directions. In the long run it may be recorded that these cartoonists were the most persuasive advocates of retention of the constitutional freedoms.

In the temper of the times it takes courage to speak up for freedom; still more to take a stand. To our great good fortune, there have been those who were willing to stand. Sometimes the deed was in the nature of a gesture, which is perhaps what should be said about Senator Fulbright's vote against the 1954 appropriation for McCarthy's committee, or Senator Margaret Chase Smith's declaration of conscience. Other examples are James Wechsler's willingness to debate McCarthy on freedom of the press despite all the handicaps of the rules of the hearings, Harvey O'Connor's invoking of the First Amendment before that same de facto tribunal, and the refusal of professors here and there to continue in the employ of institutions flagrantly disdainful of academic freedom.

Such actions are not to be dismissed lightly. Senators Tydings and Benton discovered that gestures hardly more emphatic were enough to put them out of office. The Hollywood Ten, not all of whom were proved or admitted Communists, found that resoluteness before the committee led to fine and imprisonment and to permanent disbarment from their work, or, as Dalton

Trumbo's experience seems to indicate, to less regular work at much less pay. A number of the teachers who resigned in protest, for principle as they measured it, surrendered their careers as well as their jobs.

In the familiar context of conviviality, the toast "strike a blow for freedom" commonly leads to additional rounds. Similarly, in the hard realities of our contested liberties, one noble gesture is seldom the end of it. The striking of one blow, the making of one brave stand, usually leads to further engagement. No doubt many of those who took the first brave step did so with no more than a vague realization that the repercussions might go on indefinitely. Others more consciously enlisted for the duration.

Certain organizations as well as individuals have rallied to the support of the freedoms. One is the American Civil Liberties Union. In the tradition set by Roger Baldwin the union poises itself like a volunteer fire brigade ready to rush to the defense of the rights and liberties guaranteed in the Constitution. Its primary method is by legal action, entering pleas and briefs as friend of the court and in some cases becoming the active litigant.

Practically every American indorses the theoretical desirability of the civil liberties to which the Union and the United States are committed. A whole school of thought, or rather of action, maintains, however, that exceptions have to be made, that instances arise—sometimes many of them—when these high principles must be set aside and someone's, always someone else's, civil liberties must be denied. The Civil Liberties Union's election of the case method brings it into sharp conflict with this more complacent view, which in effect holds that exceptions are not to constitute precedents, that the guaranties can be snapped off and on like a light, and that what is really wanted is a retention of the freedoms not as a guaranty to all persons but on a selective and discriminatory basis.

The case method involves further unpopularity because it tries to bring the freedoms out of the abstract and into the concrete. The work of the American Association of University Professors for academic freedom and tenure will illustrate. In operation the association avoids litigation and does not even enter as friend of the court, but like the Civil Liberties Union, it comes down to specific cases in which particular scholars have been treated as though they were incompetents or felons or subversives or worse. Its clients thus have been put under a cloud, and that is what the association also has to brave as it goes to their rescue. The same experience has been in store for the Friends Service Committee, the Anti-Defamation League, the National Association for the Advancement of Colored People, and most other organizations that have sought to be more than pontificating bystanders.

Throughout the five years after its establishment in 1952 the most resplendent champion of the freedoms was the Fund for the Republic, a fifteen-million-dollar creation of the Ford Foundation. The Fund concerned itself with assaults on academic freedom, due process, and minority rights and with censorship, boycotting, blacklisting, and application of guilt by association. Directly or through other agencies it promoted research on many facets of these problems. By awards and citations it honored organizations and individuals for stalwart work in support of the freedoms. Certain friendly cynics spoke of it as too little and too late, but the Fund stood as a symbol and a morale-builder for all friends of the freedoms.

The Fund also drew hostile fire. McCarthy blasted it, and so did Walter, Eastland, and Reece. The congressional investigators staged one-sided hearings airing charges against the Fund and then adjourned before any real rebuttal could be put into the record. A sector of the press gleefully spread the charges. Following this drumfire of criticism the directors of the Fund transformed it into a more self-contained study group with its sights trained mostly on background and theory. Nevertheless, the continued existence of the Fund for the Republic is an important asset.

A small segment of the press has gone down the line for the freedoms, upholding their guaranty to persons who are unpopular as well as to those in the bosom of the majority. Justices William O. Douglas and Hugo Black dissented on the Smith and Feinberg decisions even when the hysteria was at its height. On the air until his physician called a halt, Elmer Davis dealt bluntly with the devices of calculated expediency through which the freedoms were being jeopardized. The Alsops and A. M. Schlesinger, Jr., took issue with the Atomic Energy Commission on the walling-off of Oppenheimer. When the going was toughest, Eric Sevareid stepped forward and paid sincere tribute to John Paton Davies, and Judge Luther W. Youngdahl held the line against the palace prosecutor.

These and other articulate defenders of the freedoms were willing to stand up and be counted and at the same time could express what it was they stood for and why. Sometimes they came in for calumny because they spoke, as well as for retribution because they stood; yet the opportunity to be heard was in some degree a compensation.

They also serve who only stand. The names of these silent defenders are soon forgotten or perhaps were never known. Their role characteristically was to perform without panoply of war and, perhaps alone on a particular battleground, to brave oath, subpoena, false accusation, smear, citation, blacklist, fine, imprisonment, or disgrace. These unheralded warriors are not least among the heroes in the cause of freedom.

In spirit they are akin to the stouthearted men of Aragon, whose pledge to their king ran, "We, who are as good as you, swear to you, who are not better than we, to accept you as our king and sovereign lord, provided that you observe all our liberties and laws; but if not, then not."

Soldiering for freedom presents much that is baffling. Only at rare intervals is there a leader such as Jefferson who charts a clear course. Almost never is there a high command to issue detailed instructions. Disciplined and compact phalanxes are not the order either, but instead the greatest part of the defense is intrusted to individuals scattered all over the land. Each one, furthermore, has to wrestle it out with his own conscience whether to stand and, if so, how.

One widespread misconception about the freedoms is that they are nurtured on the blood of the martyrs. If the span is extended as far as Socrates, yes. But on the American scene the inspiration almost always has come from a stand that succeeded. Peter Zenger not only stood for freedom of the press, but made his point, and thereby is memorable. Patrick Henry's "Give me liberty or give me death" is the more inspiring because liberty was achieved. In the national anthem there is uplift because the opening question, "O say can you see?" has the happy answer that the colors have not been struck. Even the Douglas-Black dissents in the earlier civil liberties cases became more fortifying reading when the Warren court in 1957 took substantial steps toward giving body once more to the guaranties as set forth in the Constitution.

That is not to say that no stand should ever be made unless success seems certain. Honor and integrity may call for resistance even when the outlook is not favorable. On top of that, the outcome is seldom completely predictable. In the future as in the past, those who take up the gage for freedom will have to accept uncertainty as to what the result will be. This much does seem clear: for freedom's welfare there is less virtue in courting martyrdom than in exerting every effort to carry through to victory. That maxim, in turn, is not to be corrupted into a readymade excuse for abandoning the fight for freedom. Because they have, they say, no ambition for martyrdom, many at the first reason for pessimism give up the contest. The record is littered with instances of such abandonment of fields that in fair likelihood could have been held. Obviously these ignominious surrenders are no service to the cause.

Fortunately there are satisfactions. Gerald W. Johnson had them in mind when he wrote: "Whether enough of us are worthy of our inheritance remains to be seen, but some are; and for the high-hearted successor of the men of old, there is wonder in being American; for the bold man, there is delight."

11. In the Bloodstream

In *But We Were Born Free*, in 1954, Elmer Davis summed up the contemporary plight of the freedoms with a chapter heading, "Through the Perilous Night." For the freedoms the early fifties had been a time of darkness, marked by many instances of actual violence to them and ominous with portents of more dangers to come. The phrase, therefore, rang true. It contained, however, an undercurrent of optimism. In the physical world nights do come to an end, even the longest of them. The night which Francis Scott Key immortalized not only ended but broke into a glorious new day. Through this perilous night of ours Davis thus dared to hope.

The fall and winter of 1954 and the early months of 1955 brought signs of light on the horizon, and from time to time volunteer watchmen announced the dawn. Whether it was the real light of day or only a false dawn, time alone would tell. Meanwhile, there was the sobering thought, almost never voiced but inescapable, that the day would surely be perilous too.

The principal sign of improvement at that time was the turning against McCarthy. After gingerly side-stepping earlier proposals, the Senate was confronted by Senator Flanders' resolution for censure. It referred the resolution to a committee, where many thought it would be safely buried. Under the chairmanship of Senator Watkins of Utah, this committee, however, proved surprisingly resolute. Brushing aside McCarthy's challenges and protest, it went ahead with its work and, shortly before the elections, reported a resolution of censure.

The Senate narrowed the charge. By amendment it compromised out any reference to McCarthy the investigator and kept only the part that dealt with McCarthy the contemptuous senator. For his unbecoming conduct toward Senate committees and fellow senators it did vote condemnation. Strict constructionists held that this sort of rebuke would be meaningless. They emphasized that the word "censure" was not in the resolution as finally passed. The net effect, however, was salutary.

The election returns contributed a further sting. McCarthy had referred to the 1954 vote as a referendum on whether he should continue as chief investigator. The voters, nevertheless, returned a Democratic Senate as well as House, which meant that he would be relegated to a lesser role.

Observing that reporters ceased noting his every utterance, that other names got the headlines, that others replaced him in the cartoons, and that the television cameras turned elsewhere, one wit offered the slogan "Joe has gone." In a measure it was true. In fact, however, he was still in the Senate, still on the investigating committee. He was not completely silenced and in a few months would be renewing his tirades. Nevertheless, his potential to damage people and influence policy was much reduced.

The months that followed were a rugged time for McCarthy. Many old friends deserted him; the President, once glad to accept his electioneering, pointedly closed the doors of the White House. In natural reaction to the way in which McCarthy had claimed the limelight, critics and opponents now chose to make him the scapegoat for all that had been done under the banner of McCarthyism. A brush-off undoubtedly more painful came from the news-vendors. Reporters, columnists, editors, commentators, and analysts who had been hanging on his every word and press release suddenly deserted him. He had suffered a setback, but the pall of silence was so extensive as to resemble or suggest a conspiracy. At the least, the publicists who had built him up let him fall.

On top of all these discouragements McCarthy was a sick man and several times had to be hospitalized. Two factors misled the public. With friend and foe alike he had a reputation for toughness. His conduct as senator, committeeman, and campaigner had also spread abroad the impression that he was an exaggerator. For these reasons and perhaps others the public at large was not prepared for the news on May 2, 1957, that he had died.

At Washington and Appleton full honors were paid the man who just over seven years earlier had taken up the political standard of anti-Communism and almost at once had eclipsed all other leaders in the program, part crusade and part vendetta. Senator Malone proposed that the Senate expunge the vote of censure. Others voiced unstinted praise. Certain erstwhile partners praised him guardedly for his dogged fighting qualities, and a number of consistent critics found compliments to bestow—Eleanor Roosevelt, for example, credited him with being sincere.

In this book hardly a good word will be found for McCarthy. He is seen primarily as an opportunist, who in time probably made progress toward convincing himself and thus might be called sincere. But his actions throughout, including those that damaged him, bore the stamp of political calculation. And as here measured, the consequences to the national welfare and to the freedoms are seen as undilutedly harmful.

Nevertheless, it is both unjust and inaccurate to hold McCarthy solely responsible for all that happened or to assume, now that he is gone, that McCarthyism will cease to be a program or a problem. On this point, the national record since the time of his eclipse in December, 1954, is depressingly instructive. At that time one phrasemaker put forward the thought that McCarthyism had turned to McCarthywasm, but the aphorism was more clever than correct. To far too great an extent it identified with this one man the whole onslaught on dissent, nonconformity, and the freedoms. And it was much too premature in assigning this tendency and practice to the past tense.

The courts, it is true, handed down a number of decisions favorable to the freedoms. In the Nelson case a state enactment was set aside because it invaded the federal prerogative of dealing with possible subversion. In the Slochower case all the justices agreed that the inference of guilt was not to be drawn from an invoking of the Fifth Amendment. In other cases there were rulings that at least part of the questioning by congressional committees had been unauthorized and improper and that witnesses who declined to answer were not in contempt. Still other decisions struck down state actions disbarring lawyers who had invoked the Fifth Amendment. None of these decisions of 1955–56 was so dramatic as the unanimous opinion that Warren wrote calling for desegregation of the schools. The immediate effect of that decision was to concentrate attention on civil rights—rights in which all minorities should share. Violent resistance in Tennessee and Kentucky in 1956 and collateral difficulties in Alabama, followed in 1957 by the provocative interference by the governor of Arkansas, made the issue of fair treatment of the Negro the most compelling on the nation's agenda. In time the gains achieved for civil rights might well spread to the broader field of civil liberties.

Among the lawmakers, likewise, the freedoms got less rough treatment in 1955–56. Congress passed no law that went beyond the radicalism of the Humphrey Amendment. The Washington legislature considered but did not adopt a proposal for a second venture with an un-American activities committee. The California legislature rejected proposals to require non-Communist oaths from realtors, professional wrestlers, and all other persons licensed by the state. It also refused to require that churches and every other organization in the state exact a non-Communist oath from every candidate for membership. Elsewhere the pattern was the same, with few such repressive measures being introduced and fewer still enacted.

Meanwhile, an increasing number of persons spoke out against the excesses and the outrages committed in the name of anti-Communism. The American Academy of Political and Social

Science chose "Internal Security and Civil Rights" as the theme for its national convention in April, 1955. The literature of protest against encroachments on the freedoms was strengthened with books such as Telford Taylor's *Grand Inquest* and Corliss Lamont's *Freedom Is As Freedom Does*, while the protective feature of the Fifth Amendment was indorsed at book length by Dean Erwin N. Griswold of the Harvard Law School and in eloquent articles by Attorney Joseph N. Welch.

These were favorable omens, but at most they amounted to a slowing of the drive against the freedoms. They did not reverse its direction, much less repair the damage that had been done. Meanwhile, new episodes gave additional evidence of the freedoms and fair treatment being sacrificed in the name of or on the pretext of security.

The Department of Agriculture and the President took alarm at the presence of Wolf Ladejinsky in its office for land reform in Japan. His work there had been outstanding, but he had relatives behind the Iron Curtain. His writings had been vigorously anti-Communist, but Secretary Benson discounted them on the score that no one with relatives in Russia would write that way except by permission. The allegations were reminiscent of those against the Air Force reserve officer, Radulovich, who had been given an eleventh-hour reprieve. Ladejinsky was salvaged by another government agency for work in Indochina, but Benson remained adamant that his decision had been correct.

On grounds that were different but by methods that were equally highhanded, the State Department got rid of Edward J. Corsi, who had been brought in with such fanfare to try to make the refugee admissions provisions of the McCarran-Walter Act actually function.

The State Department also cashiered career diplomat John Paton Davies. The base charge against him was that a decade or more earlier he had advised that the Chinese Communists had better prospects of controlling China than did Chiang Kai-shek. On this account Davies was subjected to repeated loyalty checks and investigations, some nineteen to be exact, the net result of which was his clearance. When Secretary Dulles, however, ordered the issue reopened, Davies in weariness resigned his post.

The Department of Justice, meanwhile, continued to press for a perjury verdict against Owen Lattimore. On May 2, 1953, Judge Luther W. Youngdahl had dismissed the principal counts in the original indictment. His ruling was upheld, 8 to 1, by the Court of Appeals. Instead of going to trial with the shreds that were left of the case, the government returned to the Grand Jury and got a new indictment of Lattimore as a "follower of the Communist line," whereas before he had been called a "sympathiser with Communist interests." Learning that Youngdahl would again be the judge, the Department of Justice in almost unprecedented fashion filed an affidavit charging that he had shown personal bias and asked that he disqualify himself. Youngdahl denounced this move as "scandalous" and an attempt to intimidate the court. He kept the case. To no one's surprise, since the new indictment was almost a facsimile of the old one, on January 18, 1955, Youngdahl dismissed the new counts. The prosecution again served notice of appeal. As previously tested in court, the government's evidence appeared to be dubious and flimsy; yet all along the Department of Justice had shown itself intent on discrediting Lattimore. To prolong the case by holding at least some indictment open appeared next best to a conviction. Finally in June, 1955, the government gave up, withdrew its appeal, and quashed all charges.

Similar prolonged harassment was applied to Val Lorwin, a one-time employee of the State Department. On most inadequate evidence he was charged with having been a Communist. He contested this charge and it was dropped, but because the accusation had been made he was classified as ineligible for reemployment. Entering into litigation for reinstatement and recovery of salary, he was thereupon confronted with an action alleging perjury. The government case was woefully weak and eventually abandoned. One functionary of the Justice Department is quoted as saying that it had been easier to bring suit than to withstand the pressure from a Senate committeeman.

Early in 1955 the Eisenhower administration gave out a new score card on security separations which ran the total to 8,008. The old ambiguities persisted about how many were reckoned disloyal, how many were discharged, and how many left without any awareness that they were regarded as security risks. The Attorney-General and his special security assistant proposed slight changes, and the testimony on this proposed legislation had its surprises, notably Scott McLeod's assertion that he could conceive of circumstances in which the State Department would employ a security risk, even a Communist, in order to carry out its larger responsibility of getting its work done. The Brownell-Tompkins proposals, however, were to perpetuate the most objectionable features of the program as it had operated—the denial of the right to confront accusers and of any real opportunity for appeal.

Another phase of the work of the Department of Justice was brought to the headlines in February, 1955, by one of the department's most used informers. Ex-Communist Harvey Matusow sensationally proclaimed that as a witness for the government in a wide variety of anti-Communist actions he had lied and had lied by prearrangement with counsel.

His revelations did not differ in kind from what had been proved years earlier against informer George Hewitt in the case of Melvin Rader of Seattle. Similar doubts had arisen about the testimony of Manning Johnson. Another principal informer, Paul Crouch, had reacted to aspersions on his performance by denouncing the Attorney-General and demanding a congressional investigation. Two informers who were used against Edward Lamb in the challenge of his license from the Federal Communications Commission also recanted and admitted they had testified falsely. The Matusow disclosures thus did not stand alone.

The impulsive response in government circles was to say that Matusow's retractions were part of a diabolical Communist plot, and that those who urged reopening of the cases in which he had testified were voicing the Communist line. Matusow's word, by itself, did not establish whether his falsification was in his original testimony or in his retractions. It was enough to demonstrate that, time and time again, the Department of Justice had put forward a paid and presumably expert witness whose veracity was not to be depended upon. The Attorney-General, however, resisted all efforts to reopen cases in which Matusow had been used. Rather than pinning down the point of perjury, the department procured a three-year sentence for contempt of court. It was for retracting testimony that had aided in the conviction of Clinton Jencks of the Mine, Mill, and Smelter Workers Union.

This reaction of the Department of Justice did not dispel the possibility that Jencks was the victim of a miscarriage of justice. In 1957 the Supreme Court so ruled, setting aside his conviction on the score that the defense had not been accorded adequate opportunity to challenge the reliability of the government witnesses. The untrustworthiness of the department's favorite witnesses extends the doubt to other parallel cases. It particularly clouds a great many of the adverse decisions by the Immigration Service, where the department's professional informers, or paid experts, have been the chief reliance.

In logic, the doubt must extend also to much of the testimony, especially the naming of Communists, that has gone into the security files of the executive departments, the congressional committees, the corresponding state agencies, and even the FBI. The paid informers have been busy here too. Along with them were the secret informers, the "faceless witnesses," who could accuse without fear of cross-examination and who were protected in anonymity. The safeguards against unreliability from such sources are even less than with the open testimony of the Hewitts, Johnsons, Crouches, and Matusows.

There have been other episodes. The Post Office Department, it is revealed, has been systematically protecting American readers by refusing delivery of the Soviet dailies *Pravda* and *Izvestia*. In Boston alone, according to the Boston *Post*, it has burned tons of printed matter, including Quaker and pacifist literature and magazines containing criticism of United States actions in Guatemala, along with much that has come from Russia.

Congressman Carroll Reece, with the support of a complacent majority, conducted a highly distorted hearing on alleged support of subversion by tax-exempt foundations. He closed the hearings abruptly before the foundations had more than a token opportunity to answer the charges made. A running fire of objections by Congressman Wayne L. Hays irritated but did not deter Reece. In its majority report, early in 1955, the committee found that the foundations are "an intellectual cartel" using public money to suppress freedom and to influence academic and public opinion in a leftist direction, and that certain of their actions have been "subversive." To the thoughtful this report was neutralized by its heavy load of bias. It was available, however, as ammunition for wandering critics, and it was so used by Westbrook Pegler in an April address to a convention in San Francisco. A similar hit-and-run hearing was conducted by the Un-American Activities Committee of the House in the fall of 1956. The committee allowed time for the airing of charges against the Fund for the Republic but not for the presentation of evidence in rebuttal.

In March, 1955, months after McCarthyism was supposedly dead, the president of the University of Washington vetoed an invitation to J. Robert Oppenheimer to come to the campus for a series of lectures. The University of Oregon, it is true, promptly scheduled him for an appearance, and in 1957 Harvard invited him to be visiting lecturer. A formidable protest movement arose against the Washington action. Other speakers declined invitations, a conference of scientists had to be canceled because so many would not attend, the student paper took up the cudgels, and the faculty at length forced through a revision in the method of selecting and inviting lecturers, but without getting the invitation to Oppenheimer renewed.

In January, 1955, a still more significant exhibit had been added to the list of proofs that McCarthyism was marching on, with or without its titular leader. In Chicago the government procured a conviction of another Communist for violation of the Smith Act. His conviction was newsworthy because it was under a different clause in the statute. Eighty or a hundred party leaders had been sentenced earlier for organizing to conspire to advocate at some future date the violent overthrow of our government. Now came a conviction for joining a group that had been organized to conspire to advocate at some future date the violent overthrow of our government. Once again no semblance of an overt act was proved or even charged, and this person was still another step removed from this nebulous act that at some future date might allegedly become overt. The significance of this new tactic was soon demonstrated. When the first of the "first-string" Communist leaders emerged from prison after serving their sentences for "organizing to conspire to advocate, etc., etc.," they were rearrested to stand trial for "joining an organization to conspire to advocate, etc., etc." Perhaps the courts would see this as double jeopardy. Perhaps they would find that this provision of the act of 1940 qualified every member of this least popular political party for a term in jail. In October, 1957, the Supreme Court set aside the Chicago conviction, but on a basis that left the fundamental question unanswered.

After Russia ceased to be our ally and particularly after 1950, the domestic program of anti-Communism featured wholesale abridgments of the freedoms. Typical elements have been short cuts through due process, the penchant for fixing guilt by association, a shifting of the burden of proof to the accused, substitution of legislative exposure for trial at court and of private vengeance for official punishment, an exaltation of the professional informer and the wiretapper, revival of the medieval test oath, the myriad forms of censorship and suppression of dissent, an ever mounting stockpile of laws to enforce conformity, and a series of court decisions narrowing individual rights hallowed in custom or in the Constitution.

Many of these things, it is true, were done in the name of anti-Communism but with ulterior or partisan design. Ostensibly, however, the target has always been that paragon of disrespect-ability, the American Communist. Because he was the target, we have been asked to tolerate the crude methods that stretched the law, violated it, or went beyond it. When it was objected that these vigilante and police-state methods victimized more non-Communists and anti-Communists than Communists, the standard answer was that such casualties were regrettable but unavoidable. The apologists for the drive also insist that its measures are merely for the emergency. Once the American Communists are eliminated, they say, the committees can be disbanded, the lists retired, the dossiers put into inactive storage, the repressive enactments repealed, and other elements of the program dismantled.

This prediction may come true. The Sedition Act of 1798, because it was not renewed, did cease to be part of the law of the land. After the subsidence of the IWW, the criminal syndicalism laws became dead letter, subject, however, to revival. In the Braden case in Kentucky in 1955, where the real objection was against the sale of a white-neighborhood house to a Negro, the old criminal syndicalism law was dusted off and made the basis for prosecution. Yet it cannot be denied that particular varieties of hysteria can become passé; presumably evolution, if not UNESCO, can be taught without repercussions practically anywhere in the nation today.

Undoubtedly the most encouraging developments for civil liberties of the whole postwar era came on June 17, 1957, when the Supreme Court handed down a cluster of decisions. In the case of the fourteen California Communist leaders who had been convicted under the Smith Act for conspiring to advocate at some future time the violent overthrow of the government, the court acquitted five and remanded the other nine for possible retrial but only on the charge of outright advocacy and teaching. In the Watkins case it reversed a conviction for contempt of Congress by a committee witness who had testified freely about himself but had refused to testify about others. In the Sweezy case it set aside a New Hampshire conviction for contempt in refusal to answer questions in an interrogation by the state attorney-general. And in the John Stewart Service case it ordered reinstatement of a State Department officer, six times investigated and six times cleared but on a seventh review reported as a loyalty risk and thereupon fired. These four cases touched the key areas of prosecutions under the Smith Act, compulsion of witnesses before congressional investigating committees, state participation in ferreting out and punishing subversives, and the loyalty-security programs as set up and administered by the federal executive.

True enough, in each of these cases the court adhered to a custom of the judiciary by resting its decision on narrow grounds. As to the dismissal of Service it held that the standing regulations of the State Department interposed "substantive and procedural" limitations on the "absolute discretion" granted by law to the Secretary of State to dismiss whenever he deemed it advisable in the interests of the United States. In the Sweezy case the court held that the legislature itself could determine what facts it needed in order to legislate to combat subversion but that it could not delegate this task to the attorney-general. In the Watkins case the defect noted was that the congressional committee had not sufficiently defined the purpose of the investigation to give the witness a fair opportunity to know whether he was within his rights in refusing to answer certain questions. In the California case the reversal was because the trial judge had not properly distinguished between abstract advocacy of forcible overthrow and advocacy of action to that end.

In the opinions in support of these decisions the court spelled out its reasoning in considerably greater detail. In the Sweezy opinions, for instance, Warren and Frankfurter explicitly insisted that academic freedom must be upheld, that to "impose any straitjacket upon the intellectual leaders in our colleges and universities would imperil the future of our nation." Warren's opinion for the court in the Watkins case covered an even broader canvas. Harking back to Stuart England he reviewed Anglo-American experience relative to the powers of Parliament and Congress and the necessary limitations thereupon. In the

United States in the decade following World War II he re-marked a new phase in legislative inquiry, "a broad-scale, intrusion into the lives and affairs of private citizens," frequently subjecting these citizens to "public stigma, scorn and obloquy." The First Amendment guaranties are then described in a fashion that would seem to assure that they are adequate protection against congressional probing such as was directed against Watkins. "We have no doubt," Warren said for the court, "that there is no congressional power to expose for the sake of exposure." In the end, however, the setting aside of the conviction was based on the due process clause and the failure of the committee to let the witness know explicitly its jurisdiction and legislative purpose.

The Hearst headline for this news was "COMMUNISTS SCORE GREATEST VICTORY," while the Cleveland *Plain Dealer* said, "Well, comrades, you've got what you wanted. The Supreme Court has handed it to you on a platter. Come and get us." The attorney-general of New Hampshire opined that the Supreme Court had set the nation back twenty-five years in its fight on subversion. An Alabama congressman said he feared the Supreme Court "as presently constituted" more than he feared Russia, and a Georgia colleague rated its "steady and insidious erosion of all protective safeguards against subversion" as far deadlier than the hydrogen and atomic bombs. "What this country needs," chimed in Senator McClellan, "is a Supreme Court of lawyers with a reasonable amount of common sense." So ran the more irresponsible criticism, shortly to be summed up in formal resolution by the American Bar Association in convention in London.

A few civil libertarians went to the other extreme and exulted that the witch hunt was over, the torch of liberty relighted, and the ancient prerogatives of the Bill of Rights fully restored. The actuality was far more moderate and modest. These decisions do temper certain excesses of government. They may represent a turning of a corner, as every optimist must hope. They do not dismantle the whole machinery or countermand the whole program under which the civil liberties have been so substantially abridged. Indeed, it would have been most extraordinary for any court to sweep aside so broadly implemented a policy.

Even with these heartening rulings and some earlier decisions in which the courts found flaws in some of the more inept and discriminatory restraints, it is still pertinent to ask what freedom-violating components of the anti-Communist apparatus have been eliminated. The White House has announced that the security scrutiny of federal employees will concentrate on those in sensitive positions. Also in 1957 an unclaimed Oscar in the motion-picture academy awards revealed a hole in the Hollywood blacklist. Apparently there have been clandestine, cut-rate purchases of scripts from some of the banned writers. In the main, however, the program of bartering the freedoms in the hope of gaining security carries on.

There has been no repeal of the Smith Act, the McCarran Acts, the repressive parts of Taft-Hartley, of the Humphrey Amendment, New York's Feinberg Act, or any of California's array of similar enactments. As the contempt action against Arthur Miller illustrates, the congressional investigators still are intent on gathering names of possible Communists and possible associates with Communists. On the marrow of these decisions the House Un-American Activities Committee staged a hearing in San Francisco that was in the worst tradition. Neither the suicide of a reluctant witness nor the rules of the House as communicated by Speaker Rayburn deterred Chairman Walters from televising the hearings. They were patently designed to rebuke the California Bar Association for its temerity in censuring the committee for gross discourtesy to counsel in the course of hearings in Los Angeles a few months earlier. The committees, the FBI, the security sections of departments and bureaus, and corresponding agencies in several of the states continue to assemble dossiers on unorthodox political activities. By oath and elaborate questionnaire entering servicemen are measured against this yardstick. Through oaths and membership checks many branches of public service and in some states all public employees are similarly blanketed. The practice has also spread to many phases of private employment. With negligible exceptions, wherever this system of control has been set up it continues to function.

The publicity about this screening was mostly confined to the time when it was set going and applied to the whole body of persons at work in the specified places. Some quit rather than submit to such treatment and others were dismissed. These things made news. The stage was soon reached, however, when all currently at work had met the test of conformity or submission and firings practically ceased. It came to be understood, too, that only those willing to take a test oath or willing to be circumscribed as to political activity need apply. Except where the draft or compulsory military training in the schools threw out a dragnet, incidents and open protests became rare. Yet the tens of millions of job opportunities thus fenced off and still fenced off are a most powerful deterrent against excursions into nonconformity.

Much of the freedom-hampering factor in our striving for security thus has been institutionalized and continued in full effect. That was the clear hazard inherent in the program and is its natural upshot. Even though zeal for the crusade may fall off, the momentum and the channeling will keep the program going.

It was much less generally recognized that indulgence in this frenzy would debase the national conscience. To find that disrespect for the freedoms has become ingrained, that a public tolerance has developed for many elements of McCarthyism, that much of its doctrine is now taken for granted—such an awakening is more surprising and infinitely more alarming. Yet now it can be seen that this is where the excesses of anti-Communism as practiced in the United States exacted their final accounting.

A special demonstration occurred in California in 1954 when the churches and related groups had to decide how to respond to the requirement of an oath of denial as the price of continued enjoyment of tax exemption. In many communions there was much soul-searching. Some thirty fellowships filed a public protest along with the required sworn statement, but only twelve out of twelve thousand congregations refused to execute the oath. Some of the protests were explicit as well as emphatic in asserting the civic damage entailed in loyalty oaths. The most memorable words of all were in a communication considered but not sent by the YMCA at California Institute of Technology: "We commend ourselves to all who read this letter as a demonstration of the erosion of freedom. We are less than free, and less than men. But we are tax exempt."

Another exhibit was at Seattle in the summer of 1954 when the Velde committee came to town to hear a paid witness name some three hundred residents as Communists, former Communists, or fellow travelers. The overwhelming public reaction was to acclaim the performance. Citizens, clubs, unions, civic bodies, and fraternal groups deluged the committee with congratulatory messages. There was a general movement to drop those named from office or membership, to fire them from their jobs, and in many instances to discharge close and collateral relatives as well. This was at the very time when the Army-McCarthy hearings were allegedly debunking the reckless inquisitor, but public sentiment in Seattle appeared to be wholeheartedly in support of the ministrations of Velde.

At about the same time a committee of scientists headed by Samuel A. Stouffer was analyzing nationwide sentiment on these same issues. Through an elaborate and double-checked opinion poll Stouffer's committee found that the majority of Americans not only wanted all Communists excluded from "sensitive" work such as defense plant jobs and college teaching but in addition wanted them barred from other work such as clerking in a store or singing on the radio. Communists, they also said, should be barred from speaking, should have their citizenship taken away, and should be put in jail. The majority likewise approved reporting suspected neighbors and acquaintances to the FBI, wiretapping to get evidence on Communists, punishing the witness who declined to answer, and hunting out all Communists even though some innocent people are hurt.

The modern willingness to carry out a pogrom against the American Communists discards practically every guaranty in the Bill of Rights, not only the assurances of free speech and a free press, but the promises of presumption of innocence and that even the lowliest individual can count on fair and personal trial. It is a complete departure from what the Founding Fathers bequeathed us. This attitude, instead, is one that we have created for ourselves, mostly in the period since the Second World War and primarily in our efforts to dispose of the handful of American Communists. Anti-Communism thus expressed became, in many respects, the most powerful force in our thinking. It is our generation's contribution to the American heritage. Because its tendency is to make regimentation and police-state methods more commonplace, it stands as an incubus on the American future.

Even before the Warren court moved to renew the strength of the constitutional guaranties of freedom, there were astute observers who thought that popular opinion had taken a decided turn. They sensed a general disillusionment with a security program leaning so heavily on silencing dissent and using so many unscrupulous methods. Improving on the theory that "the Supreme Court follows the election returns," some of these analysts accounted for the Jencks, Watkins, and Sweezy decisions by saying that the justices were responding to this change in the climate of opinion. They saw the decisions as portending other steps in a quick revival of enthusiasm for the old-time freedoms.

This optimistic view has strong appeal and some supporting evidence. There is, first, the undeniable fact that when McCarthy was forced into retirement no comparable fire-eater arose to take his place. The "Indian Charley" tactics that he had boasted of went out of style, and several of his cronies campaigned in 1956 in a manner quite reformed. The tempo of adding new curbs on the freedoms certainly has slackened and on most fronts no new methods or devices have been brought forward. It may be, also, that some of the old machinery grinds more slowly.

Yet the conditions that called forth the hysterical retreat from the freedoms still exist. Instead of fading away, Soviet Russia kept on making herself a more and more formidable adversary. Her prowess in atomic science and the steady buildup of her submarine fleet and long-range bombers kept the pressure on our defense efforts. Then in the fall of 1957 the breakthrough into outer space and the demonstrated superiority of Russian rockets put us in still greater peril. The Russians, furthermore, match us in intransigence. The net result is that we have more reason to be jittery about exposure to attack than at any time during the Cold War.

Nor has the American Communist advanced a jot toward popularity or acceptance, and though less numerous he is by no means extinct. The habit of viewing this minority as a fifth-column nest of enemy agents is still strong. Popular attitude can change—we have, for example, done a rapid about-face from our wartime distrust of the Germans and Japanese—but there is nothing to indicate that we are more reconciled to the American Communists than when the Stouffer survey took the national temperature on this issue in 1954. The fever started up in the early postwar years and climbed more rapidly with the spy trials and the Korean War. So little room was left for it to go higher after 1954 that this curve had to flatten out, but there is little to indicate that it has dropped appreciably.

Conceivably we might be as exercised as ever about containing the Communist minority, but determined now to do it without violating or sacrificing the freedoms that are the American birthright. Yet when one looks for actions in which any such sentiment has been put into operation, hardly a one can be found. What law has been repealed, what administrative order retracted, what nonconformist voluntarily restored to his position, what blacklist discarded? More broadly, what freedom is now demonstrably more secure than it was when McCarthy was in full voice? Except as the Supreme Court decisions of 1957 made marginal changes, such as requiring more personal proof for conviction under the Smith Act, the evidence of improvement is as yet most intangible.

Even the civil liberties affirmations of the Warren court drew an edgy comment from President Eisenhower indicating his disapproval, a blast from former President Truman, a chorus of abuse from the South predisposed against the court because of the desegregation order, and more criticism than praise from northern congressmen and editors. Not altogether the makers of public opinion, these are voices that represent it.

The future does not have to be so out of step with our traditions, not even the immediate future. Not one of our betrayals of the freedoms has been written into the Constitution. They exist by executive order, as in the Attorney-General's list; by simple precedent, as in the pillorying by the legislative inquisitors; by simple enactment, as in the Humhprey Communist Control Act; by private compact, as in the Hollywood blacklist; or by decisions of a divided court, as in the finespun opinions on the Smith Act and the Feinberg Act. Consequently, nothing so elephantine as a Bricker Amendment is needed to reverse them. We as a people have it readily in our power to take the United States back to first principles. A summoning of popular determination is all that is needed.

Selected Bibliography

Much of the comment on the state of the freedoms in postwar America has been fugitive. It has occurred in newspaper reports and editorials, in magazine articles, and in the still more evanescent form of the spoken word, with or without broadcasting. For comprehensive review one could leaf through the voluminous files of a paper such as the New York *Times* or the St. Louis *Post-Dispatch*. Analysis and commentary have been more concentrated in such periodicals as the *Nation*, the *New Republic*, *Frontier*, the *Progressive*, and the *Bulletin of the Atomic Scientists*, and in the publications of organizations such as the American Civil Liberties Union. For rapid recall nothing surpasses Herbert Block's anthologies, *The Herblock Book* (Boston: Beacon Press, 1952) and *Herblock's Here and Now* (New York: Simon & Schuster, 1955), and Daniel R. Fitzpatrick, *As I Saw It* (New York: Simon & Schuster, 1953).

The book list that follows opens with a number of general titles, listed in the order of appearance, and continues with more specialized studies, grouped by topic.

GENERAL

Robert E. Cushman, *New Threats to American Freedoms* (Washington: Public Affairs Committee, 1948) and O. John Rogge, *Our Vanishing Civil Liberties* (New York: Gaer Associates, 1949) sounded an early warning on the erosion of the freedoms in the postwar mania for security. That was the theme also of Carey

193

McWilliams, *Witch Hunt* (Boston: Little, Brown & Co., 1950). Written before McCarthy had gained much headway, it deals more with Dies, J. Parnell Thomas, Truman's loyalty program, and the aping of this program in states, schools, and industries. Its theme is that the modern drive differs in detail but not in essence from the persecution by the inquisitors and witch hunters of old.

Writing in part from direct knowledge gained as Attorney-General, Francis Biddle in *The Fear of Freedom* (Garden City, N.Y.: Doubleday & Co., 1951) dissects "the contemporary obsession of anxiety and fear in the United States." He charts much of the historical background and is at his best in appraising the consequences to American justice that flow from anti-Communism as it came to be practiced in the United States.

The Loyalty of Free Men (New York: Viking Press, 1951), by Alan Barth, is a journalist's thoughtful discussion of the problems of loyalty, the repressive approaches that have been used, and the alternative method which would put the stress, as does the book's title, on the loyalty of free men.

Henry Steele Commager, *Freedom, Loyalty, Dissent* (New York: Oxford University Press, 1954) offers a group of essays, some written as long ago as 1947, in which a most competent historian advances the proposition that preservation of the freedoms through their actual exercise is imperative. Elmer Davis, *But We Were Born Free* (Indianapolis: Bobbs-Merrill Co., 1954) is likewise essentially a gathering of speeches and papers previously delivered to audiences and editors. What gives it unity is the crackle of Davis' personality, remembered from his broadcasts and imbedded in the fearlessness with which he writes.

Perhaps in an excess of zeal to defend the fair name of Socialism, and despite his own qualification that "men are often better than their creeds," Norman Thomas in *The Test of Freedom* (New York: W. W. Norton & Co., 1954) accepts the conspiracy doctrine and holds it applicable to all Communists. He would go only halfway in blanket proscription of the American Communists. He would protect their right to public speech but not to private speech; and he would countenance them in the arts and professions but not as teachers. Yet in the application of any of these disbarments, the label of Communist is all the evidence he would require. If that is conceded, little more remains than to quibble about how much penalty to assess.

More than any of the foregoing, Corliss Lamont, *Freedom Is As Freedom Does* (New York: Horizon Press, 1956) is a testament of personal experience by one who has dissented sufficiently to be caught up in some of the pressures for conformity. It also achieves a broader résumé of happenings on the entire civil liberties front.

BACKGROUND AND THEORY

Morton Grodzins, *The Loyal and the Disloyal* (Chicago: University of Chicago Press, 1956) and John H. Schaar, *Loyalty in America* (Berkeley: University of California Press, 1957) probe the meaning of loyalty and the problems attendant on efforts to measure or enforce or insure it. William O. Douglas, *An Almanac of Liberty* (Garden City, N.Y.: Doubleday & Co., 1954) has a simpler approach. Its 366 pages have a short essay for each day of the year. For them Douglas has ranged through American and English history and beyond for episodes illustrating the real meaning of every aspect of our liberty. Continuity is sacrificed in the day-book form, but the almanac brings out forcibly the interrelations of the freedoms. Leon Whipple, *The Story of Civil Liberties in the United States* (New York: Vanguard Press, 1927) proceeds with little elaboration through a long calendar of challenges of the freedoms.

Zechariah Chafee, Jr., *Three Human Rights in the Constitution of 1787* (Lawrence: University of Kansas Press, 1956) stresses the English backgrounds of rights specifically covered in the Constitution. On the principal cluster of these guaranties see Robert Allen Rutland, *The Birth of the Bill of Rights* (Chapel Hill: University of North Carolina Press, 1955) and Edward Dumbauld, *The Bill of Rights and What It Means Today* (Norman: University of Oklahoma Press, 1957).

James Morton Smith, *Freedom's Fetters* (Ithaca, N.Y.: Cornell University Press, 1956), John C. Miller, *Crisis in Freedom* (Boston: Little, Brown & Co., 1951), and Claude G. Bowers, *Jefferson and Hamilton* (Boston: Houghton Mifflin Co., 1925) report the first great endangering of these principles through the Alien and Sedition Acts. Another epoch of challenge in the interval between the two world wars is surveyed in masterly fashion in Zechariah Chafee, Jr., *Free Speech in the United States* (Cambridge, Mass.: Harvard University Press, 1941). Specific parts of this story are enlarged upon in Robert K. Murray, *Red Scare: A Study in National Hysteria, 1919–20* (Minneapolis: University of Minnesota Press, 1955) and Eldridge F. Dowell, *A History of Criminal Syndicalism Legislation in the United States* (Baltimore: Johns Hopkins Press, 1939).

THE INVESTIGATORS

August Raymond Ogden, *The Dies Committee* (Washington, D.C.: Catholic University of America Press, 1945) is a carefully documented and judicious appraisal of the work of the Committee on Un-American Activities through the seven years of Dies's chairmanship. The judgment, succintly put, is that the means were not justified. William Gellermann, *Martin Dies* (New York: John Day Co., 1944) is a biography based on the public record: the *Congressional Record*, the published reports of the committee, and the newspaper stories and editorials. Of Dies, Gellermann is a dispassionate but severe critic.

Robert K. Carr, *The House Committee on Un-American Activities, 1945-50* (Ithaca, N.Y.: Cornell University Press, 1952) is an expanded sequel to Ogden's book. Here too the record dictates the conclusion that the achievements of the committee are considerably outweighed by its mistakes and abuses. In general, it would appear, this same analysis would hold for the committee since 1950. One salient of this committee's activity is elaborated from a different perspective in Gordon Kahn, *Hollywood on Trial: The Story of the Ten Who Were Indicted* (New York: Boni & Gaer, 1948).

Other books study antisubversive actions by several of the states. Lawrence H. Chamberlain, *Loyalty and Legislative Action* (Ithaca, N.Y.: Cornell University Press, 1951) covers the work of the New York legislature from 1919 to 1949. Edward L. Barrett, Jr., *The Tenney Committee* (Ithaca, N.Y.: Cornell University Press, 1951) gives a faithful and noncommittal review of the hearings, pronouncements, and reports of the California committee erected in the image of Dies's committee. The final chapter is mildly critical of the committee's standards of evidence and procedure. In 1947-48 the state of Washington had a similar committee in the field. Vern Countryman, *Un-American Activities in the State of Washington* (Ithaca, N.Y.: Cornell University Press, 1951) demonstrates the wisdom of the legislature in letting this committee lapse. Walter Gellhorn (ed.), *The States and Subversion* (Ithaca, N.Y.: Cornell University Press, 1952) takes stock of loyalty and security measures instituted in six other states and the problems thus generated.

IN THE ERA OF MCCARTHY

McCarthy: The Man, the Senator, the Ism (Boston: Beacon Press, 1952), by Jack Anderson and Ronald W. May, is a most revealing account of McCarthy's rise to power. Its is the basis for most subsequent writing on his deeds and misdeeds to 1952. The special book-length issue of the *Progressive* for April, 1954, McCarthy: *A Documented Record*, goes rapidly over the ground covered by Anderson and May and pursues the trail through another twenty-four busy months, up to but not including the Army-McCarthy hearings. It is a frank and unanswerable exposé, though McCarthy tried in a freely distributed booklet, *McCarthyism: The Fight for America*, and William F. Buckley, Jr., and L. Brent Bozell entered the lists as special pleaders with their *McCarthy and His Enemies* (Chicago: Henry Regnery Co., 1954). Special pleading for McCarthy's expulsion from the Senate characterizes Sherman Ford, Jr., *The McCarthy Menace* (New York: William Frederick, 1954). James Rorty and Moshe Decter, *McCarthy and the Communists* (Boston: Beacon Press, 1954) is more restrained but unqualifiedly hostile.

The weekly essays in which Michael Straight covered the Army-McCarthy hearings for the *New Republic* were republished, somewhat revised, as *Trial by Television* (Boston: Beacon Press, 1954). There is a literature also of report by persons subjected to interrogation by the committeemen. Owen Lattimore, in *Ordeal by Slander* (New York: Bantam Books, 1953), recounts his bouts with McCarthy, McCarran, and others. James A. Wechsler, *The Age of Suspicion* (New York: Random House, 1953) includes a recital of his colloquy with McCarthy. G. Bromley Oxnam, *I Protest* (New York: Harper & Bros., 1954) follows a churchman's tangle with the House Un-American Activities Committee. Philip Wittenberg (ed.), *The Lamont Case* (New York: Horizon Press, 1957) transcribes with commentary the official documentary record of another long-drawn-out affair before a committee, the Senate, and in court.

Fear, the Accuser (New York: Abelard-Schuman, 1954), by Dan Gillmor, is constructed on a formula only slightly different. By quoting extensively from their sittings, it reveals what the congressional investigations have been doing. The picture is sinister. Telford Taylor, *Grand Inquest* (New York: Simon & Schuster, 1955) also analyzes the congressional investigations. With a lawyer's bent, Taylor searches out the origins of a number of matters both integral and collateral—how parliamentary investigations came into being, the derivation of the privilege against self-incrimination, and outlawry and why it was abandoned.

THE LOYALTY-SECURITY PROGRAM

Eleanor Bontecou, *The Federal Loyalty-Security Program* (Ithaca, N.Y.: Cornell University Press, 1953) describes the federal loyalty

197

program as initiated by President Truman, scrupulously giving it the benefit of every doubt, yet finding more to criticize than to commend. A report of a special committee of the Association of the Bar of the City of New York, *The Federal Loyalty-Security Program* (New York: Dodd, Mead & Co., 1956), brings the Eisenhower version of the program under scrutiny and is even more critical. A briefer treatment is John Lord O'Brian, *National Security and Individual Freedom* (Cambridge, Mass.: Harvard University Press, 1955). For a recent review holding out little hope for further curbs by the courts, see David Fellman, "The Loyalty Defendants," *Wisconsin Law Review*, January, 1957. At note 9 he cites many other articles. With anonymity to shield the individuals involved, Adam Yarmolinsky, *Case Studies in Personnel Security* (Washington, D.C.: Bureau of National Affairs, 1955) describes a hundred cases and their disposition. In "Security Measures and Freedom of Thought," *Yale Law Journal*, March, 1952, psychologists Marie Jahoda and Stuart W. Cook assess the personal effects of the federal program.

In the Matter of J. Robert Oppenheimer (Washington, D.C.: Government Printing Office, 1954), a 992-page release by the Atomic Energy Commission, gives the transcript of the hearing before the Personnel Security Board. The findings and recommendations appeared separately, as did the decision of the commission, the texts of which are available in *U.S. News and World Report*, July 9, 1954. In the *Atlantic* for October, 1954, Arthur M. Schlesinger, Jr., brilliantly assessed the processes and the results. In *Harper's* that same month Joseph and Stewart Alsop were even more caustic. Their article provoked a denunciation from the Atomic Energy Commission, which *U.S. News and World Report* published, December 24, 1954, along with rebutting comments from the Alsops. The Alsops expanded their initial article into a book, *We Accuse* (New York: Simon & Schuster, 1955). A painstaking dissection of the whole procedure, not at all flattering to Oppenheimer's judges, is Charles P. Curtis, *The Oppenheimer Case* (New York: Simon & Schuster, 1955).

Using specific examples, Milton R. Konvitz, *Civil Rights in Immigration* (Ithaca, N.Y.: Cornell University Press, 1953), demonstrates how far the McCarran Acts and administrative decisions pursuant to their philosophy have closed the gates to potential immigrants, meanwhile greatly increasing the liability of residents to denaturalization and deportation.

On the FBI there are two principal references: a rather morose critique by Max Lowenthal, *The Federal Bureau of Investigation* (New York: William Sloane Associates, 1950), and Don Whitehead's paean of press agentry, *The F.B.I. Story* (New York: Random House, 1956). The discerning reader will discover that they are about the same organization and have significant points of agreement. Lowenthal's concern is more with the bureau's impact on the freedoms; Whitehead's book outcirculated its rival, fifty or a hundred to one. Scholars and the public have had very few glimpses into the FBI files. We must hope that Harvey Matusow, *False Witness* (New York: Cameron & Kahn, 1955) does not report an average cross-section. In *Harper's* for March, 1954, Alan Barth raises the question, "How Good Is an F.B.I. Report?"

THE CONSTITUTIONAL YARDSTICK

Under our traditional doctrine of judicial review, actions of citizens and of the various branches of government can be brought to final accounting before the Supreme Court, which will measure them against the ultimate yardstick of the Constitution. Some actions are never called to this accounting and on others the review is delayed until they have run their full course. Nevertheless, this area is a most important one. In *Bill of Rights Reader* (Ithaca, N.Y.: Cornell University Press, 1954) Milton R. Konvitz reproduces opinions and dissents pronounced in some eighty recent Supreme Court cases in which civil rights and liberties were involved. Some passages are bogged down in the jargon of the law; others rise to eloquence. The significance of this judicial discourse, however, is that it presents the thinking at the level where for this given time the effective meaning of the Constitution is determined. C. Herman Pritchett, *Civil Liberties and the Vinson Court* (Chicago: University of Chicago Press, 1954) analyzes the division and opinions on every case from 1946 through 1953 in which a civil liberty was at issue. A basis is thus afforded for assessing the outlook and performance of individual justices and of the court as a whole. There is information about trends and some suggestions why the court permitted so much diminution of traditional freedom. In time, similar studies no doubt will be made of the Warren court and its work.

Although many constitutional issues pertinent to civil liberties have arisen in the postwar era, the one most widely debated has concerned the Fifth Amendment's ban against forced self-incrimination. On the popular front the argument against the amendment has been headed by Sidney Hook in two books, *Heresy, Yes—Con-*

199

spiracy, No (New York: John Day Co., 1953) and *Common Sense and the Fifth Amendment* (New York: Criterion Books, 1957). The first identifies the Communist party in the United States as a conspiracy and argues that the conspiratorial characteristic is the dominant mark on every party member; membership thus becomes prima facie evidence for exclusion from positions of trust or sensitiveness such as those of teaching. The second goes all the way in approving the inference of guilt whenever there is refusal to testify. Although thinking the amendment not at all necessary to assure fair trial, Hook is willing to permit continuation of the privilege as an archaic carry-over in court. But he condones the congressional investigator and urges the professions and the public to interpret any such refusal to testify as an admission of guilt.

There is a contrary view. It is presented tellingly in Erwin N. Griswold, *The Fifth Amendment Today* (Cambridge, Mass.: Harvard University Press, 1955). Telford Taylor's *Grand Inquest* summarizes the historical background. A particularly illuminating article is Norman Redlich and Laurent B. Frantz, "Does Silence Mean Guilt?" *Nation*, June 6, 1953, and a more technical discussion is Leonard G. Ratner, "Consequences of Exercising the Privilege against Self-incrimination," *University of Chicago Law Review*, Spring, 1957.

ACADEMIC FREEDOM

Richard Hofstadter and Walter P. Metzger, *The Development of Academic Freedom in the United States* (New York: Columbia University Press, 1955), following the method of history, carries the story to about 1920. Using the approach of sociology and philosophy, Robert M. MacIver, *Academic Freedom in Our Time* (New York: Columbia University Press, 1955) carries on toward the present.

Through the guise of describing the philosophy and functioning of an ideal university in an ideal society, Robert M. Hutchins, in *The University of Utopia* (Chicago: University of Chicago Press, 1953), sets forth his firm ideas about the need of both society and the university for uninhibited thinking. One of the most thoughtful of today's college presidents, Harold Taylor, in *On Education and Freedom* (New York: Abelard-Schuman, 1954), tackles several controversial issues, including the most vexing one—how the colleges should guard against being made sounding boards for Communist propaganda.

Articles on academic freedom have appeared in a great many publications—for example, Robert P. Ludlum, "Academic Freedom and Tenure: A History," *Antioch Review*, Spring, 1950; "The Integrity of the University," *University of Chicago Round Table*, October 21, 1951; Monroe E. Deutsch, "Let There Be Light," *Pacific Spectator*, Winter, 1952; and Joseph Alsop's open letter to the Harvard Overseers, *Atlantic*, June, 1953. In particular see the *Bulletin of the American Association of University Professors* for such articles as Robert M. Hutchins, "The Freedom of the University," Summer, 1951; John W. Caughey, "Trustees of Academic Freedom," Autumn, 1951, and "The Practical Defense of Academic Freedom," Summer, 1952; Alexander Meikeljohn, "The Teaching of Intellectual Freedom," Spring, 1952; and Charles I. Silin, "The Clear and Present Danger," Winter, 1953.

In support of its action in disciplining six alleged Communists or ex-Communists or fellow travelers, the administration of the University of Washington issued a 125-page brochure, *Communism and Academic Freedom* (Seattle: University of Washington Press, 1949), which includes the committee reports and the president's recommendations to the Board of Regents.

The early phases of the oath controversy at the University of California are dealt with sharply in Dixon Wecter, "Commissars of Loyalty," *Saturday Review*, May 13, 1950, and by George R. Stewart and his collaborators in *The Year of the Oath* (Garden City, N.Y.: Doubleday & Co., 1950), which unfortunately stops short of the actual firings. The issues are well defined in a pamphlet by an alumni committee, *To Bring You the Facts* (Berkeley, 1950) and in two other pamphlets, [Alexander Meikeljohn], *Crisis at the University of California* (San Francisco, 1949 and 1950). For a brief narrative that reaches beyond the dismissals see John W. Caughey, "A University in Jeopardy," *Harper's*, November, 1950. The further ramifications are best covered in the briefs of attorney Stanley A. Weigel in *Tolman v. Underhill*, a suit which led to invalidation of the university's special test oath requirement, and, in 1954, in twenty-one suits asking payment of accrued salaries or of severance pay as promised. See California, 3 Civil No. 7946; as reviewed by the Supreme Court, Sac. No. 6211; and Superior Court, Sac. Nos. 96371–96391.

A report by a special committee of the American Association of University Professors, published in the *Bulletin*, Spring, 1956, surveys and analyzes the impact of anti-Communist activities upon higher education in the United States. A score or more of specific incidents are appraised and a formulation of standards is attempted.

ATTITUDES AND SANCTIONS

A scientific inquiry into American attitudes relative to the freedoms was one of the projects sponsored by the Fund for the Republic. Samuel A. Stouffer, *Communism, Conformity, and Civil Liberties* (Cambridge, Mass.: Harvard University Press, 1955) reports the results. The fact of widespread willingness to sacrifice the freedoms in hope of gaining security is confirmed. That community leaders showed considerably more tolerance was another finding.

A couple of years earlier Merle Miller investigated the degree to which "listing" in *Counterattack* or *Red Channels* was a bar to employment in the entertainment industries. His conclusion in *The Judges and the Judged* (Garden City, N.Y.: Doubleday & Co., 1952) was that the blacklist really worked. Elizabeth Poe, "The Hollywood Story," *Frontier*, May, 1954, reported similar effectiveness at the West Coast studios. Another Fund for the Republic project led to John Cogley's *Report on Blacklisting* (2 vols.; New York: Fund for the Republic, 1956), which adduced abundant evidence on the effectiveness of blacklisting in the motion-picture industry and in radio and television. There was a kickback through summonses and leading questions by a congressional investigating committee, none of which tarnished the validity of the report.

CREATIVE WRITING

Perhaps because the imputed conflict between security and the freedoms is too difficult to resolve, there have been few attempts to treat this theme in verse or fiction. May Sarton, *Faithful Are the Wounds* (New York: Rinehart & Co., 1955) deals with the trauma of Harvardians under the heel of a congressional inquisitor. Martha Dodd, *The Searching Light* (New York: Citadel Press, 1955) follows a university community demoralized by an oath requirement. Abraham Polonsky, *A Season of Fear* (New York: Cameron Associates, 1956) is a study of character disintegration in the wake of a loyalty check and purge in the personnel of a public works project. In *The Un-Americans* (New York: Cameron Associates, 1957) Alvah Bessie, one of the Hollywood Ten, agonizingly re-creates the tensions that surrounded an indictment and prosecution for perjury. Significantly, in three of these four novels, the character study focuses on a non-Communist liberal and his loss of self-respect and integrity as he accommodates himself to the dictates of conformity. A more eloquent statement is a portfolio of verse by John Beecher, *Land of the Free* (Oakland, Calif.: Morning Star Press, 1956).

Index